PRAISE FOR **Two Weeks Notice**

'My only regret is that this book wasn't around when I started as an entrepreneur. It might have saved me from a bunch of bumps and bruises. Amy does a remarkable job breaking down the steps for creating a passion-filled life and business. If you're a woman dreaming of breaking through the glass ceiling to create a life on your terms and enjoy the process along the way, this book is exactly what you need.'

Mel Robbins, *New York Times* bestselling author and award-winning podcast host

'Ready to ditch your 9–5 and follow your dreams? Then get this book now! In her signature step-by-step style, Amy delivers a practical and inspiring blueprint to becoming your own boss.'

Marie Forleo, #1 *New York Times* bestselling author of *Everything Is Figureoutable*

'Amy unveils the mindset, skill set and grit required to quit your job and unboss with clarity. Not only will you find the courage to give your two weeks' notice, but this book will guide you step by step through navigating entrepreneurship with a greater sense of peace, purpose and freedom.'

Patrice Washington, host of *The Redefining Wealth Podcast*

'If you're looking for a book that will change your life, this is it. *Two Weeks Notice* is for dreamers and doers looking to create a life and build a career that lights them up. Through honest accounts of her own experiences and an unmatched ability to help others design their futures, this book will be your roadmap to step into your true entrepreneurial calling. Inspiring, beautiful and actionable. The adventure awaits!'

Jenna Kutcher, *New York Times* bestselling author of *How Are You, Really?* and host of *The Goal Digger Podcast*

'If you've been daydreaming of starting your own business and being your own boss but have no idea where to start, this book is just the motivation you need. Entertaining and incredibly inspiring, it's packed with actual practical advice that will set you up for major success.'

Alli Webb, president of Canopy
and founder of Drybar

'*Two Weeks Notice* is the solution for any woman craving more out of her life and career. With its insight grounded in research and Amy's real-life experiences, you'll feel empowered to say "Yes!" to your own entrepreneurial journey and to create a life of impact, time and financial freedom. This book will crack you open to the infinite possibilities of what life can be without a glass ceiling.'

Gabrielle Bernstein, #1 *New York Times* bestselling
author of *The Universe Has Your Back*

'If you know you were made for more but don't know what that more is or how to get there, Amy takes you by the hand and gives you the tools, the courage and the roadmap to help you step into your destiny! Get ready – this just might be one of the most important rides of your life!'

Jamie Kern Lima, *New York Times* bestselling author
of *Believe It* and founder of IT Cosmetics

'Amy was one of the first people to paint a brighter future different from my present reality, but she didn't just share her ideas... she gave me her exact steps. This book unlocks a clear path to starting a digital business and also empowers you to push fear aside to step into your destiny.'

Jasmine Star, creator, podcaster
and CEO of Social Curator

'There's one word to describe this book: FINALLY! You'll finally have the opportunity to pursue your dream and escape the rat race, and you'll finally have a clear and solid plan right in front of you.'

Pat Flynn, bestselling author of *Will It Fly?* and *Superfans* and host of the *Smart Passive Income* podcast

'This book made me want to start my business all over again because it's so inspiring and practical. Amy's the best teacher I know in this industry, and this book is gold if true freedom is your desire!'

Kate Northrup, bestselling author of *Do Less*

'Amy Porterfield is the TRUTH! She has put together the most practical guide to building an online business that helped me personally in a major way. This book is everything I wish I'd had when I traded in the "employee" title for "entrepreneur."'

Anthony O'Neal, CEO, author and speaker

'From setting non-negotiables to "you're not for everyone, boo" to unbossing, the book made me feel seen and equipped me with the tools to improve my craft. Even as an experienced course creator, the book was extremely helpful.'

Teri Ijeoma, founder of Trade & Travel

'A stunning example of what's possible when you dare to dream big. This book is a call to action for anyone who's ever felt like they were made for more.'

Ed Mylett, author of *The Power of One More* and peak performance expert

two weeks notice

two weeks notice

FIND THE COURAGE TO
QUIT YOUR JOB,
MAKE MORE MONEY,
WORK WHERE YOU WANT
AND CHANGE THE WORLD

AMY PORTERFIELD

HAY HOUSE

Carlsbad, California • New York City
London • Sydney • New Delhi

Published in the United Kingdom by:
Hay House UK Ltd, The Sixth Floor, Watson House,
54 Baker Street, London W1U 7BU
Tel: +44 (0)20 3927 7290; Fax: +44 (0)20 3927 7291;
www.hayhouse.co.uk

Published in the United States of America by:
Hay House Inc., PO Box 5100, Carlsbad, CA 92018-5100
Tel: (1) 760 431 7695 or (800) 654 5126
Fax: (1) 760 431 6948 or (800) 650 5115; www.hayhouse.com

Published in Australia by:
Hay House Australia Ltd, 18/36 Ralph St, Alexandria NSW 2015
Tel: (61) 2 9669 4299; Fax: (61) 2 9669 4144; www.hayhouse.com.au

Published in India by:
Hay House Publishers India, Muskaan Complex, Plot No.3, B-2,
Vasant Kunj, New Delhi 110 070
Tel: (91) 11 4176 1620; Fax: (91) 11 4176 1630; www.hayhouse.co.in

Text © Amy Porterfield, Inc., 2023

Cover design: Briana Summers and Julie Davison • *Interior design:*
Lisa Vega • *Interior photos/illustrations:* Amy Porterfield, Inc.

The moral rights of the author have been asserted.

A catalogue record for this book is available from the British Library.

Hardback ISBN: 978-1-78817-821-1
E-book ISBN: 978-1-78817-823-5
Audiobook ISBN: 978-1-78817-822-8

Printed and bound in Great Britain by
TJ Books Limited, Padstow, Cornwall

Hobie, you have always thought of me as a "big deal"
even when there was little proof.
Thank you for believing in me from the start,
especially in the early years when I rarely believed in myself.
I love you.

Contents

You Call the Shots

Fourteen years ago I walked into a meeting with my boss at the time, peak performance coach Tony Robbins, and a group of top-tier online entrepreneurs. Tony was looking to launch his products online in a bigger and more strategic way and wanted to learn from the best. The results didn't disappoint: right there in our San Diego office sat a dozen of the number one experts in creating, scaling, and growing online businesses.

While today I might have been invited to that meeting as one of the experts, back then I was just a member of the content team who had been brought into the meeting to take notes. Little did any of us know the domino effect that meeting would have on my life.

One by one, the men around the table—and the experts were all men—began to tell their stories. This one had built a business around dating tips. That one had started a business sharing stock market strategies. A third had built a business educating would-be real estate investors. As different as their businesses were, there was one word their stories all had in common: *freedom*. Financial freedom. Lifestyle freedom. Creative freedom. But always *freedom*.

The word rang in my ears. My heart began to beat faster. I had never once entertained the idea that I could call the shots in my own career. The thought of it was exhilarating to me. To work when I wanted to work, how I wanted to work, and where I wanted to work? All thanks to this online business model they were teaching us?

I have no idea how they're doing what they're doing, I thought to myself, *but I want a piece of it.*

I'd never thought much about online marketing before. While I was taking notes, I wasn't really taking *in* what they were talking about. Sitting in the corner of that room, my mind was spinning on one single thought: I was not currently free. It dawned on me that maybe I never *had* been. These men were charting their own paths, creating value in the world on their own terms. Me? I had been following a script for my life designed by someone else entirely. I wasn't even sure who had written the script I was following, but it sure wasn't me. One thing was clear: I would do just about anything to change my circumstances. From that day forward, I was on a mission to figure out how to be the boss of my own life. Which meant, first and foremost, becoming the boss of my own business.

The challenge? I had no freaking idea how to do it. There was no guidebook, no college course, no real training for how to launch your own online business. Worse yet, I didn't see any women doing it. But even back then I knew I didn't want to follow the path the men before me had paved. I wanted a business that suited *all* of me and my unique challenges, attributes, and life experiences as a woman.

While there are many people out there claiming to teach the art of launching an online business, I've found that most books are far too general. "Start a business." "Come up with a great idea and test it." "Build a following." Advice like this will only keep you dreaming and dabbling. It's too vague; it isn't rooted in a proven process that has already been used thousands of times to build real businesses. And it doesn't provide the practical framework that you need to actually and concretely get started. In addition, building a business is a balance between strategy and mindset. I can give you all the strategies you need to succeed (and I plan to do so!), but if you are not mindful of your thoughts and feelings throughout your business building journey, you are setting yourself up for a whole lot of frustration and overwhelm.

I know this from personal experience. I was that girl in the cubicle who knew I was made for more but for years was too afraid to admit it. I was too scared to make a change; too insecure to believe I could really do it. Then, once I finally mustered the courage to give notice at my stable job, I was on my own. It felt like trying to build a skyscraper without blueprints. Enter: years of embarrassing failures and crippling self-doubt. I fell flat on my face more times than I can count. Which is why I'm writing this book: to give you the road map I didn't have. To walk you through the mindset shifts *and* step-by-step practicalities that come after you take the leap and give your notice. To help you start your own online business, become your own boss, and make more of an impact—and more money—than you've ever imagined.

I've created eight successful digital courses and a top-ranked podcast helping women build online businesses. My journey from corporate girl to eight-figure entrepreneur includes more messy ups and downs and painful lessons than I'd care to admit. But it's all been worth it—because now I get to show *you* how to do the same.

I was 31 years old when I left my final nine-to-five job to start my own business. Before that I held countless jobs, with positions ranging from an event planner for a nonprofit organization, a sales coordinator in the publishing industry, and a marketing manager for Harley-Davidson dealerships. I've had a lot of jobs to say the least and all of them, for better or worse, helped prepare me for my wildest adventure into becoming my own boss.

In my business today, through a mix of mindset shifts and proven marketing strategies, I teach budding entrepreneurs how to find the courage to take the leap into starting their own business. Once they've taken the leap, I teach them modern marketing strategies focused on list-building, email marketing, online launching, and digital course creation to help them create thriving, profitable businesses. I've been able to create a multimillion-dollar business because I started with a strong, clear foundation that was deeply rooted in my values, skills, strengths, and purpose.

After many false starts, major fumbles, and painful lessons, today my life is exactly what I've designed it to be. I am a woman who calls the shots. And thanks to starting my own business teaching online marketing, I have time for the things that matter most and the means to do the things I want to do. I only work on the projects that light me up; I take vacations when I want and for as long as I choose; and I have the financial means to live where I want and contribute to the causes I care deeply about. And most importantly, I understand from the inside what it means to have the kind of freedom those men had been talking about in that conference room over a decade ago.

My deep desire is to see more women—marginalized women, women of color, women of all economic backgrounds, religions, and sexual orientations—hold more positions of power, call the shots, make more waves, make more money, and pave their own way, on their terms. I believe we *can* build these better futures—futures that demand the respect, recognition, and freedom we all deserve—for ourselves and the women who will follow in our footsteps. Together, supporting each other, we can turn the glass ceilings we've crashed into time and again into the floors on which we stand.

THE PROBLEM—AND THE SOLUTION

Let's face it: even in this current day and age, gender equality in the workplace is still out of reach for many. Women make up 47.7 percent of the global workforce,[1] but only 6.4 percent of CEO roles at S&P 500 companies.[2] Men are promoted at 30 percent higher rates than women during their early career stages.[3] Women are paid 82 cents on the dollar of their male colleagues, and it's even worse for women of color, who make as little as 71 cents to each of their white male colleagues' dollars.[4] And 50 percent of women in STEM fields eventually leave their jobs because of hostile work environments.[5]

It's no wonder that women working all different types of jobs—from teachers to therapists to service providers to corporate managers—feel stuck, underappreciated, uninspired, overworked, and underpaid. The answer to this problem is not as easy as finding a new job. Things might get better for you in the short term, but over time the frustration and dissatisfaction slowly come creeping back in.

If you feel stuck, you are not alone. I was exactly where you are right now, stuck in a situation I desperately wanted out of, but also feeling completely confused as to how to make a shift. What I learned then is that creating your own online business is the ultimate solution. And it's the only *real* solution—because it allows you to be your own boss, call the shots, and become untouchable from gender gaps, glass ceilings, and hostile workplaces.

When I talk about "creating your own business," I'm talking about living a life by your own design—creating something that sparks joy for you, impacts lives, fosters creativity, and allows you to control your financial future. Your life will be dramatically different when you begin to live by your own rules and call the shots the way you see them.

After working with tens of thousands of students—mostly women—I've discovered the two big challenges that often stand in the way of taking the big leap to decide to be your own boss. First, you must find the courage to admit you're unhappy where you are and that you want more. The second challenge is not knowing where to start.

It took me years to admit to myself that I wanted a better work life. Each time I dared to dream of being my own boss, I would instantly think, *That seems too risky. What if I crash and burn? Besides, I have a great job. It's stable. What if I can't make any money? I should be grateful! Plus, I don't know enough to go out on my own. What if I have to beg for my job back?*

This immobilizing self-doubt keeps a lot of women from going after their dreams. But what I've seen is that the origin of this fear is not based in reality—it's actually about something much deeper. Deep inside, so many women believe that we are not good enough, talented enough, smart enough . . . heck, the list of "not-enoughness" can go on and on.

But what if you *do* allow yourself to take this opportunity? What if you take the stand that you *do* deserve more? What would that mean for other areas of your life? Would you start to believe you deserve more in your marriage? In your friendships? In your relationship with yourself?

And then comes the second challenge. *What are the actual steps I need to take to turn my desire for more into a legitimate business? What will people think? What would I sell? Who would buy from me? How do I grow an audience? How will I find the time to start this? Can I do it alone?* The exhausting list of unknowns is enough to send a girl straight back to her cubicle.

In this book, I provide a concrete, easy-to-follow online business start-up plan. Your journey will include the most important actions you need to take to ensure you have built a solid business foundation that you can continue to grow and scale for years to come. The goal is to do it the right way from the get-go. We will focus on the most important steps to help you take the leap from your current situation into entrepreneurship, while implementing proven strategies for success, including finding your audience, tackling social media, crafting compelling content, growing your email list, and creating profitable offers to make you money. Chapters 2 through 12 each contain a "Do the Work" exercise to give you a direct experience of progress, every step of the way.

It's the book I wish I'd had as I was desperately trying to find the courage to start my own business, filled with actionable steps as well as the encouragement you'll need to keep steady when the fears and doubts come flooding in from all sides. This isn't just a bunch of random advice; it's a blueprint I've been teaching for years, with proven results for women from all walks of life. This book, in and of itself, is a journey, and I encourage you to give yourself the time and space to implement what you learn, one step at a time. This book is not meant to be a quick read that you get through in a weekend and then move on to the next great business book on your list. If you don't give yourself the time and space to implement the strategies laid out for you, you will miss out on the magic! You've got to do the work, and I'll show you how each step of the way. Use this book as your field guide. Grab your highlighter to call out the most important sections, dog-ear the pages that speak to you the most—really sink your teeth into this experience! And remember, there is no need to rush; in fact, take all the time you need. After all, you are creating a life and business by your own design, and that kind of greatness takes time.

The end result? You—becoming your own boss. You—shattering the glass ceilings above you. You—making a bigger impact and more money than you ever imagined. You—experiencing endless possibilities and opportunities that right now might feel like a distant dream, but—I promise!—can soon be your reality.

You are wildly capable of making your dream business and lifestyle a reality. I'm going to be with you, virtually holding your hand and cheering you on the whole way.

Chapter 1

Decision Time
How to Turn Your Dreams into Your Reality

A bout six months before I left my corporate job, I had a fateful encounter with an executive in the organization. The company was growing, and as counterintuitive as it might sound, we were shutting down a few profitable lines of business to make room for the new changes. Many projects that had been planned for months had been changed or halted altogether.

Around the same time, Tony Robbins was going to be featured on the *Today* show. One thing that is unique about Tony is the way he preps for media appearances. The man does his homework. With the help of his team, he rigorously researches and prepares, not only for the interview topic, but also for the people who will be interviewing him, and even other interview guests. He cares about the entire experience and never cuts corners.

This interview was no different. Unfortunately, the team member who was supposed to be gathering all the research for this appearance had been dealing with a family emergency. When it became clear—at the very last minute—that she wasn't going to be able to support Tony, I was asked to step in. I had about five minutes to familiarize myself with the interview topic and research details and specifics of the interview when my phone rang.

It was a VP wanting to know what the interview points were, who would be interviewing Tony, and more. I was not prepared to give her what she needed and explained that I'd only been brought on this project a few minutes before.

"But you were in the content meeting yesterday, weren't you?" she demanded, frustration oozing through the phone.

"No," I replied. "I recently transferred out of the content department and moved into a new marketing role. I am on the marketing team now."

"Amy," she said. "That is ridiculous. You are *not* a marketer!"

I froze instantly. Soon tears were streaming down my face. Her words had crushed me.

I'm not sure where she was coming from that day. We were both in a tense, time-sensitive situation, and she was confused as to why I was in a marketing role when she had only ever known me in content. But the truth is, it really doesn't matter what she meant because the point of this story is *what I made her words mean*—and how it almost derailed my entire entrepreneurial journey. I turned "You are not a marketer" into *You are worthless* and *You will never make it on your own* and *Who do you think you are?* I could have let these thoughts—and that moment—change the trajectory of my plan. But I didn't. Instead, I saw it as my "nudge from the universe" to make a new decision, and that's exactly what I did. I instantly doubled down on my exit strategy and used that experience as fuel to keep going.

My students tell me similar stories. Janine's moment of clarity came after she had spent six long, tedious months working on a specific campaign—which had included weeks spent in a hotel room, many missed family events, including her daughter's big dance recital, and more anxiety than she had ever experienced before. Then she read in an email (that she just happened to be cc'd on) that the project was canceled and the campaign was moving in a different direction. Instead of focusing on all of her lost time and added stress, she promptly opened up her calendar and chose her exit date (something I will teach you how to do in Chapter 2!).

After building a career for more than three decades, Anne's opportunity to choose a new path came the day she was called into her boss's office to be told that her corporate position had been eliminated. Three years later, Anne was *still* trying to land another corporate gig when her husband turned to her and said, "You know, sweetie, you were meant for something better than this." She decided to take the leap and follow her dream of creating her own business, The Pattern Design Academy®, a program for people who want to explore the online art field and are figuring out what's next in their lives.

Sue had been out of the workforce for seven years, raising her babies while her partner worked full-time. When she was ready to work outside the home again, she couldn't believe how much the world had changed. She got her opportunity to make a new decision after a series of terrible interviews for jobs she didn't even want, where she'd be working for people less experienced than her. She decided that was *not* going to be her reality. Although she was terrified to go out on her own, her gut told her to build her own business. Today, Sue successfully owns an education-and-training company focused on women and investing.

If any of this sounds familiar to you, you're in the right place. Working for yourself means never facing these humiliating, degrading, and frustrating moments again. It also means you get to experience a totally different type of life, one that allows you to design your work around what matters most to you. It also means that, at least in the beginning, you'll work harder than you've ever worked in your entire life. But trust me, it will 100 percent be worth it.

So the first step is to *decide* you're going to do this. If you weren't up to it, I don't think you'd be reading this book. But you have to choose for yourself. Remember, saying yes to creating your own business doesn't mean you won't have doubts, fears, and worries about your future or your ability to pull this off. Saying yes just means you believe in yourself—and your ability to build a business— just a *little bit more* than you don't.

And a quick side note: If you've already quit your job or have been taking time off—or if you already have a business but *still* feel like you're working for others—you're in the right place. You might be a little farther down the path of your entrepreneurial journey, but if you're like me and most of my peers, you started off without a guidebook. That means you might have missed a few important steps along the way, making it more difficult for you to see the kind of impact and revenue you set out to create. If that's the case, use this guide with a beginner's mind and allow yourself to go through each of the steps, triple-checking that your foundation is solid and fully optimized to generate the kind of success you deserve.

ARE YOU THE ENTREPRENEURIAL TYPE?

At its heart, mine is the story of a little girl who *wanted* to be told what to do.

It started with my dad. I grew up in Southern California, and when I tell you that my family was blue collar to the core, I mean it. My dad was a firefighter, and my mom worked part-time as a hairstylist. They had a marriage that would be defined as "traditional" by most standards: My mom managed the chaos of everyday life, driving my sister and me to every appointment, recital, and playdate and making sure there was a homemade dinner on the table every night. My dad provided financially for the family and always called the shots. When I was growing up, I thought that was just the way it was—the man of the house made the most money and set the rules.

I was on a perpetual mission to impress my dad and learned very early on to be a yes-girl. It started with following his house rules—including doing my chores and never, *ever* talking back. When I showed him my straight-A report card, he would tell me how proud he was of me and take me out to a special dinner to celebrate. After college, when a report card would no longer do the trick, he was always the first call I made to share news of a raise, promotion, or award at work. He would tell me he was proud of me and we'd talk about my future and all the opportunities that lay ahead of me.

Over time, I moved from wanting to impress my dad to wanting to impress my employers. I worked late into the night, took on extra projects, and traveled at a moment's notice. I was addicted to people thinking I was "on my way up." I lived for raises, awards, and accolades. The word *boundaries* was not even in my vocabulary. I felt any *no* would be a sign of weakness, which would inevitably result in my replacement.

You need it now? Of course!

You want me to do it over, even though it took me months to perfect? You got it!

You want me to fully sacrifice my personal life and only live for work? I'm your girl!

Although I hate to admit it, I was desperately seeking validation from my bosses because I did not value or love myself. In fact, if you'd asked me back then about my inherent value as a person, I would have looked at you funny. *People have value just for being themselves?* I would have thought. *Maybe other people, but not me. My value comes from how hard I work. Did I mention I just got promoted?*

I would have liked to think I was working hard for the benefit of others. There I was, working for Tony Robbins— a coaching organization that transformed tens of thousands of lives every single year. But if I was honest, helping these people was *not* my motivation. I wasn't working my tail off to change lives, to support others in need, or to do good in the world. Nope, I was going above and beyond, overdelivering in everything I did, for one single reason: to impress my bosses. (And everyone else around me, for that matter.)

Impressing people translated into being important and valuable. I was addicted to the validation that came from working hard. Validation that came from the outside, by the way, because giving *myself* validation wasn't even on the menu.

Thankfully, an experience in my early thirties—near the end of my perpetual corporate climb—altered my course. Val, my best friend since the seventh grade, had finally found her perfect match and was getting married. It was a destination wedding, tucked away in a sleepy seaside town. A fairy tale by any measure—except my own.

Sleepy seaside town translated into only one chilling thought: no Wi-Fi. Back at work, we were finishing up a big project, and I was the one in charge of all the moving parts. I *had* to be at the wedding—I mean, I really wanted to be—but I also *couldn't* unplug.

So I hatched a plan. Between the champagne toasts, rehearsal dinners, and posing for selfies with the bride, I would secretly dash around town, hole up in the backs of cafés, and grab what Internet service I could. It would be *fine*. As long as no one from the wedding party saw me, nobody needed to know.

Or so I thought.

At the wedding reception, my best friend turned to me and said, "All you do is work." The look of total disappointment on her face is still burned into my memory. My whole body grew hot with embarrassment, and I could feel the sting of tears welling up, just one blink away. All I could say in response was, "I know." I couldn't even look her in the eye because I didn't want to confront what I knew to be true. My entire life *was* work, and I hadn't been present for all the special moments in my life.

The truth was (and still is) that hard work is how I "do life"—I will always find value in working hard, and frankly, I enjoy it. I think it's important that I own that. But at that moment, I knew something was off. Very, very off.

Did I have an aha moment, call the company, and quit in that very moment? Nope. Monday morning I was back at my desk—and right back to chasing raises, promotions, and *attagirls*. But there was a crack in my armor that would only grow wider.

In time my self-awareness grew, as did my desire for a different kind of life. Once *freedom* was on the menu, it was destined to be mine. A burning desire to be in charge grew within me until I absolutely could not ignore it. The thought of working for someone else or being on someone else's time no longer felt right to me. As I was planning my exit, I slowly shed the yes-girl identity and began to see myself as a business owner. I could feel a massive shift happening and I was ready to embrace it at any cost.

WHAT'S YOUR *WHY*?

When I ask my students *why* they want to start their own businesses, the most common responses are "I want to change the world!" and "I want to help as many people as possible!" But while I'm sure the desire to be of service factors in for many of my students, it's rarely what's *really* driving their decision to give notice. And that's just fine. Human beings are . . . wait for it . . . naturally selfish. It's what keeps the species alive, so you don't have to be ashamed of it. Your *why* does not need to be big or altruistic. The only thing it needs to be is 100 percent *honest*.

I can say this with authority because my *why* felt incredibly petty to me when I first went out on my own. It was solely focused on what *I* wanted. Or, more truthfully, it was solely focused on what I *didn't* want. My *why* went something like this: *I do not want another person to tell me what to do, when to do it, or how to do it—ever again.* That's it. That was my *why*.

To ensure that I went all in—and that there was no chance of turning back—my *why* had to be deeply personal and focused on a self-serving motivation. That way no person or outside influence could sway me or take it from me. The burning desire was mine, and it wasn't going anywhere.

I want you, too, to dig deep and get honest with yourself about why you're considering taking a leap that scares the pants right off you. If you did not care what others might think of you, what would be your true *why*? If you did not fear being judged or misunderstood, what would you admit you deeply wanted? If you were being brutally honest, what are you sick and tired of dealing with? What do you want to change? What do you want to move toward? What do you want to move away from?

My friend, what do you *really* want for you, your life, and your business? You must declare your *why*, because your honesty here will act as your anchor when things get tough. It will keep you grounded and focused along the way so that you can create a life and business by your own design.

DEALING WITH COLD FEET

The more real you get with yourself about your why, the more the worries and fears will start to pop up. But the only way I got to where I am today is by allowing my *why* to become bigger than my worries.

I am still standing today, with a multimillion-dollar business that allows me incredible freedom, not because I had the best strategy in the world. It's not because I'm the best teacher in the world, nor because I had the best marketing in the world when I started. I am standing here today because my desire to work when I wanted to work, how I wanted to work, and where I wanted to work was just *a little bit more* important to me than my fear of failure and humiliation. If you choose a *why* that's bigger than your worries, you, too, will be in this for the long game.

A known situation—no matter how frustrating, overwhelming, soul-sucking, or depleting—feels safer than an unknown future. This is why it's so easy to say, "I'm going to start my own business . . . someday." "I'm going to do what I *really* want to do . . . someday." "I'm going to make money on my own terms . . . someday." We don't fully believe in our ability to be our own boss. We are scared that if we crash and burn, we won't be able to get back up. Feeling safe feels comfortable. I get it. Better the devil you know than the devil you don't, right?

But the devil you know is still . . . *the devil*. Security tricks us into believing that we have enough and that we don't desire more—even when it's very obvious that we *do* desire more. A security mindset dims our light. It neglects the fact that we have big dreams and hopes that can only be realized on the other side of our comfort zone.

Deep down, I believe we all want freedom more than we want security. Freedom to call the shots. Freedom to make as much money as we want to make. Freedom to do what we want to do, when we want to do it, in the way we want to do it. Freedom comes with risks—it's a fact. The path to your freedom *will* at times feel like you want to come out of your skin, or at least crawl under the covers and hide. But I promise it's so very worth it.

If you are willing to push past your immediate desire for security, comfort, and certainty, you will experience the ultimate freedom of creating your own kind of security, on your terms, in your own business.

YOUR CONCERNS ARE NORMAL

Of course, there are some legit questions you should be asking yourself—having to do with logistical details like time, money, energy, and opportunity. But be careful of turning reasonable questions into unreasonable concerns. Let's walk through the most frequent concerns I hear and why they don't need to prevent you from achieving your goals.

1. **I don't know exactly what business I want to start.**
   That's okay; a "starter idea" is enough. When I left my nine-to-five job, I was not at all certain what type of business I was going to build, but I knew I could do marketing consulting to make money in the short term as I began to test the

waters. That starter idea was enough to give me the courage to leap. Even if you think you know exactly what your business is going to be, things may morph and change by year two or three. I've seen it happen time and again. You will want to decide how you will make money in the short term and how you will add value, depending on your expertise (which we will discuss in the coming chapters). But you certainly don't need a detailed business plan with specifics on revenue projections, target market analysis, and long-term growth. I certainly did not have anything close to a business plan! Do not think you have to have every detail figured out before you give notice—no one ever does.

2. **I/my spouse/my partner is worried the bills won't get paid.**
    You *will* need a financial runway—but it's not as difficult to get one as you think. I did not have a nest egg put aside when I became my own boss. My plan? To hustle. And that's just what I did, making things happen as fast as I could in those first two years. Trust me, there are many different ways you can make money on your own, right from the very start. We'll explore some options in the coming chapters.

3. **I'm afraid to put myself out there—what if I fail?**
    News flash: you *will* fail, likely many times. I have never met an entrepreneur who has not fallen flat on their face, only to dust themselves off (usually after a good cry!) and put themselves back out there. Failure is part of the process—it's how you

learn. If you are willing to mess up as you go, your dreams are already within reach.

4. **I don't have any capital to get started.**
You'd be surprised how low the overhead can be if you're working from home and starting online. Most of my client success stories are from women who did not have capital to start—they just had to be strategic to get their businesses up and running quickly. If they can do it, so can you, and I'm here to help you.

5. **I'm afraid I can't do it.**
I get it. In the very beginning, I doubted my abilities at every turn. But then I remembered that the alternative was to go back to a life that no longer brought me joy. In other words, I had no alternative. My why motivated me to put one foot in front of the other in spite of the fear. You can do the same! Plus, remember, you are not alone. You will have my time-tested, step-by-step road map for launching a business of your dreams— I've got you!

6. **When I think of going out on my own, I can only see the ways it could go terribly wrong—I can't even imagine myself succeeding.**
It is normal to look at worst-case scenarios and run through each of them. The challenge is that these scenarios (which have not even happened, by the way!) are likely on a loop in your mind, cycling over and over again—leaving no space for possibility. This is going to derail you fast. Here's what to do, starting right now. You must give "equal air time" to all the things

that could go *right*. Each time you find your-self in a thought loop of what could go wrong, stop yourself and think of one success you might have. Force yourself to look toward your future with excitement and anticipation and envision things working out, just as you have planned them.

7. **I'm afraid of what my family and friends will think when I tell them of my plans. I don't think I'll have the support I need to take the leap.**
    Oh, I've got you covered! In the next chapter we are going to dive into this very topic! It's impor-tant that you are mindful of who you share your dreams with—and who does *not* get to be a part of your journey (at least not yet). I will give you a script that you can make your own to help you navigate these important conversations so that you can find the support you need. You are not alone in this!

8. **Deep down I don't believe that I could ever make a full-time income in a business I created from scratch.**
    I'm going to let you off the hook for a moment. It's okay that you don't believe (yet!) that you can make a full-time income with your own business. Your belief in yourself and your abilities will come with time. Right now, I want you to reach deep inside of yourself and gather all the courage you possibly can to keep moving forward, one step at a time. Those steps can be baby steps, small shifts you make each day that will eventually lead you to what you really want for yourself and your life. I will take care of giving you the road map you need to

get started with your online business. As long as you lean on your courage, together we can get you where you want to go.

9. **Other people are already doing what I want to do, and they are already successful at it. There's no room for me.**

Oh, this is one of those pesky thoughts that comes up *so often* for new business owners. Telling yourself it's already been done is a sure way to keep yourself stuck. What's often underneath this excuse—because it's just that, an excuse—are the thoughts *Who am I to be doing this? I don't know enough. I am not skilled enough. I can't do it as well as they are doing it!* It's good old-fashioned imposter syndrome at its best! There are a few things I want to remind you of. First, there are 7.7 billion people on this planet. There is absolutely room for you in any niche or market you enter. Second, no one will ever create content and add value the way you specifically can, from your perspective with your voice. This world needs your special gifts, and don't ever forget it!

10. **I just don't think I am ready. Maybe I should revisit this in a year or two when my life will feel less messy.**

Have you ever heard anyone say, "There is never a perfect time to have a baby?" Well, that sentiment also rings true for starting a business. At any given moment, most of us would say that our lives are messy in at least one area, if not many! That's just the way it goes. You will never be in the perfect situation to get started. The best advice I can give you is to stop looking for the perfect moment and get started *now*. Without a doubt, if you don't get started today, a year from now you will look back and regret that you delayed your dreams.

I know it may seem too good to be true that you—yes, *you!*—could work for yourself, chart your own course, and make exponentially more money than ever before. Heck, if you're anything like I was, you might not even know what charting your own course looks like! But know this: There's something better waiting for you. There has to be. All you have to do is make the decision, say yes, and take the next step.

Just like Johnny in *Dirty Dancing*. Remember the moment when Johnny busts into the ballroom, finds Baby sitting at a dimly lit table, and says his famous line, "Nobody puts Baby in a corner"?

Think of me as your Johnny. (Not the hunky dance-instructor part, obvs, but the *effortlessly believing in you* part.) I'm standing next to your table, asking you to come dance. You may think you're who your boss says you are, who your colleagues see you as, or who your family believes you to be. But what I see is a strong, creative genius ready to step into who you are *meant* to be. I don't mean to rush you, but your audience is waiting. Come with me away from that table—your old situation that you've clearly outgrown—and courageously stride toward the stage for your moment in the spotlight. It's time to make that decision to turn your *why* into a reality. Once you do, the rest is inevitable.

Chapter 2

Unbossing
How to Give Your Notice

When my student Caroline was in the process of leaving her job to go out on her own, she found herself in a constant freeze response. Even though she'd known she wanted to quit for over a year, she just couldn't bring herself to take concrete steps forward. Every time she started to think about planning her new business, setting up a website, or designing her offer, fear rose up like a tsunami. Her main concern? Losing the financial security she'd enjoyed at this company for the last six years. There wasn't much that was steady or stable in her life growing up, and the thought of upsetting the apple cart when it came to her finances was survival-level terrifying. So even though she felt unappreciated and knew she was underpaid, she would talk herself into staying, at least for a few days. But soon enough, the end of the weekend would come, and she'd once again be faced with the "Sunday Scaries"—dreading the upcoming workweek so much, it made her queasy.

Then the company announced they were downsizing, and just like that, she was unemployed. She was also completely *unprepared*. Fast-forward two years, and today Caroline is thankful for the successful business she's built. Her only regret is not having prepared herself to leave a year earlier so that she could have given notice on her own terms, with the kind of runway that would have supported her goals.

The moral of this story: don't be like Caroline! Now that you've officially decided to unboss yourself, or in other words, *become your own boss*, there are four important steps I want you to take—starting today—so you can hit the ground running when the time comes. First, you have to choose the date you are going to quit and start your new life. Second, you have to start taking action to build your runway. Third, you'll need to tell supportive family and friends so they can help hold the vision for you. And lastly you have to give notice. (Hello, so exciting!) Ready? Let's go!

CHOOSE YOUR EXIT DATE

I live by the adage that "it's not real until it's scheduled." What I mean is that if it's not on my calendar, it's likely not going to happen. All the good intentions in the world don't matter if there is not a date and time assigned. When I need to work on a new podcast episode, the time to record it is in my calendar. When I want to plan out a new marketing campaign, you can bet the time to do so is added to my calendar well in advance. One of the most critical skills of a business owner is to take action when action is needed. Things are not going to get done only because you have good intentions. The act of planning, scheduling, and showing up to do the work are even more important than any good intentions you might have.

This is twice as true when we're talking about your departure date. Setting the date makes the whole thing real. It also avoids having one foot in and one foot out— which only causes more pain, something you may already be experiencing. When you just have a *vague* idea of when you *might* leave, you start swimming in a soup of discontent, postponement, and, at times, crushing doubt. I want more for you than that! This is your *future* we are talking about: your freedom, your happiness, your hopes and dreams. This future deserves an actual, concrete, line-in-the-sand, this-is-happening-no-matter-how-scared-I-am *date*. Trust me on this one. Your future self will thank you for this incredibly bold, courageous decision.

I know this works because I did it myself. About three months after that aha moment in the conference room—where I realized I was *not* free but really, really wanted to be—I was in my pajamas, sitting cross-legged on a beat-up leather couch in my little condo in Carlsbad, California. It was nine o'clock on a weeknight, and suddenly I was overcome with the need to make my desire *real*. It wasn't enough to just think about it or dream about it anymore; I needed to take a tangible step to bring this dream to life. I made the decision: I would quit my job on June 19, 2009. My hands were shaking as I wrote the date on a sticky note with a Sharpie and posted it on my bathroom mirror—where I could look at it every single day while I brushed my teeth and got ready for work. It was exactly the reminder I needed that this *was* happening: I was finally, truly, and irrevocably leaving my job and becoming my own boss.

If something in you freezes at the idea of getting *that* specific, you're not alone. Choosing a date can be anxiety-producing because, well, then you're *actually* leaving your job. There's no more hemming and hawing; the future has already begun.

But I want to let you in on a little secret that should ease your mind. When you choose a date, you're putting the universe on high alert. Doors will start to open;

opportunities will start to show up right in front of you. All the preparations that need to happen will start to fall into place, and on an accelerated timeline. The universe is on your side, and choosing your date and making it known is giving the signal for the miracles to enter stage left. You'll have to trust me on this one!

If you're still freaking out a little bit, I want you to close your eyes and think about the future you. Picture her: the woman who is independent, confident, scared but determined, calling the shots, making things happen, and building the business of her dreams. That version of you is ready and waiting. See her in your mind's eye. What is she wearing? What is she feeling? Where is she? What is it like for her to be free of her employer's expectations and requirements? Picture her there, creating the life and business of her dreams. Now step into her—become her, because she *is* you.

The biggest obstacle between where you are now and this future you is one tiny, little decision: On what date will you leave your current situation? Whether you've been in a nine-to-five job, a period of unemployment, or a stretch of years as a full-time mom, you wouldn't be reading this book if you weren't ready to launch a new venture that's yours and yours alone. So take a deep breath, look at the calendar, and choose a date.

Choose the month, day, and year when you will officially exit the old situation you're in and become your own boss. Will it be three months from now? Six months? Nine months? A year from now? When will it be? Choose your date.

Even if you plan to start a side hustle and spend your nights and weekends creating the business that will eventually become your full-time gig, you *still* need to choose an exit date when you will eventually go all in with your business, if that's what your goal is. I've seen too many people hold on to their full-time job while desperately wanting to take their side hustle to the next level. At some point, to fully realize your dreams, you need to go all in. Let's plan to make that happen.

To help you choose your date, here are a few questions to ponder:

- If you were your bravest self and trusted that you indeed could make this work, what date would you choose?

- If you have a time frame for your exit in mind, ask yourself if you are allowing too much time to pass before you take the leap because you are afraid of the unknown. If so, what would you need to *believe* about yourself and your situation to courageously choose a shorter time frame?

- If fear were not a factor, what date would you choose?

- Think about your *why* and then ask yourself, *How much time am I willing to let pass before I go after what I truly want?*

Now grab a sticky note and a Sharpie. Write the date on the sticky note and put it somewhere you will see every single day. I want you to remind yourself daily that you have declared your date and that your exit is happening, no matter what.

One final note: The date you choose is not as important as the act of choosing a date—and sticking to it. It might be one year from now, or maybe even a little longer, but it's happening.

Finally, look around. Notice where you're sitting. Notice the time of day, the day of the week, what season it is outside. Look down and notice what you're wearing, and look inside and notice what you're *feeling*. If you want, take a selfie right now, holding that sticky note—even if you've got a terrified look on your face.

I never want you to forget this moment, because this is the moment your entire life is changing. I want this moment to be etched into your memory so that when the future you who is living out her dreams looks back, she easily remembers the moment her new life began.

BUILD YOUR RUNWAY

Once you've chosen your exit date, it's time to create a runway that will help you move into your new reality. Your runway will consist of the specific steps you choose to take before you take the leap and make your exit. It does not need to be elaborate; in fact, the simpler it is, the better. Below I will give you a plan in the form of a checklist that you can tweak and make your own. The goal is for you to complete each action item in the plan so that you are intentionally moving toward leaving behind what you no longer want and moving toward what you do.

Now, speaking of your plan, I'd like to say that once you've chosen your date, everything will be smooth sailing. Ha! I think we both know that's not reality. When I chose my exit date, I chose a date six months out so I could be more prepared. I wanted to take some time to figure out what type of business I was going to create and to gain insight and know-how in areas I knew would come in handy. But that meant six months of working at a job *after* I'd decided to leave—super tough. It wasn't that the job was terrible, but once I'd officially made up my mind to go, I was ready to *go*.

I tell you this because choosing your exit date while still being fully immersed in your current situation is a tricky thing to navigate, both physically and mentally. You'll likely want to leave immediately, but you'll also know it's not yet time. So you have to live in this very uncomfortable place of having a foot in two worlds. But you can do it—I know you can. The way to stay productive and sane is to make a plan and then schedule it to make it real.

Once I knew I wanted to start my own business, I began to think more strategically. Due to shifts in the company, there was an opportunity for me to make a lateral move from the content department to the marketing department, and I jumped at it. I marched myself into my boss's office and asked if I could switch departments. To my surprise, she said yes. I spent the next six months actively participating in marketing projects, learning everything I could about digital courses, content messaging, and how to sell online. When my exit date came around, I was still completely uncertain about how I was going to make it all work—in fact, I was terrified. But I did it anyway, because that's what future bosses do (wink, wink).

It's important to know that you have options. Unless you threw caution to the wind and are leaving tomorrow (if so, congratulations!), you can figure out the baby steps you need to take to strategically build your momentum toward making your dream a reality. Here's a list of the things to do (and not do) as you create your own runway toward your exit date.

- *Do define your starter idea.* Remember, you don't need to have everything figured out before you begin to create your online business. No one ever

22

does! However, you at least want to have a rough idea of what your product or service is going to be so that you can start working in that direction. As you begin to take action, your momentum will lead to more clarity, which may lead you to change things up or move in a new direction. It's all part of the runway, and the only thing you need to do now is *trust the process*! And don't worry, I'll go over this in more detail in Chapter 4!

- **Do create a financial plan.** I've already shared with you that you do not need to save up a bunch of money before you begin creating your business. Because the overhead of an online business is low, you can get started right away, no savings required. However, if you need to make money from the get-go, you will want to create a temporary money-making plan as you get things up and running to support your financial goals. For me, that looked like taking on a few paying clients and helping them with their social media as I worked on my first digital course, even though ultimately I wasn't interested in a service-based business where I worked with clients one-on-one. If you aren't yet sure what your options are, hang tight— we'll be going over my favorite business models in Chapters 11 and 12.

- **Do be willing to put yourself out there.** One of the most important steps you can take as you begin to build your business is to start creating original content. You have many options to do so, including social media posts, a blog, a pod- cast, or a YouTube channel. (Psst . . . Don't worry about figuring this all out on your own, I've got you in Chapter 7.) The important thing for now is to make a conscious effort to create content so that you can get into the habit of talking about your business idea and showing up for the people you eventually plan to serve.

- **Do create your new work space.** This one is fun! Most of us just starting out will be working from home. If that's the case for you, too, it's important that you find a quiet spot in your house where you can be alone and concentrate. In the beginning you might find yourself crammed into a corner somewhere, stationed at the end of the kitchen table, or tucked away in the basement. Don't worry if you look around your makeshift office and think, *This is not what I envisioned when I dreamed about working from home!* It won't always be this way. When I was getting started, my "office" was the closet. Today, I have two spacious rooms in my Nashville house: an office designed with a coastal feel to remind me of my California roots, and a video-and-podcasting studio with every piece of equipment I need to create magic. Back in my closet days, I couldn't have imagined my home work space would ever look like this. But that's what's exciting about this journey: you never know what's in store for you. Keep going!

- **Do tell a few supportive family and friends.** In order to keep yourself accountable, I encourage you to share your new business idea with a few specific family members or friends. If you are not sure who you want to share your news with, I'll give you some guidance a little later in the chapter.

- **Don't bother creating a "traditional business plan."** If I'm being totally honest, I am not sure what a "traditional business plan" even looks like. I'll bet most of my entrepreneurial peers would say the same. Heck, one of my friends (who is now wildly successful) literally wrote some bullet points on the back of a napkin in a moment of inspiration late one night at Denny's. True story! Unless you're looking for investment capital, you don't need a fancy slide deck or anything resembling a conventional business plan. All you need is to follow a proven step-by-step guide, which you happen to be holding in your hands, and a commitment to the plan you create.

- **Don't waste time on business cards.** Oh, business cards—the first-time entrepreneur's rabbit hole of wasted time and energy! It's a rookie move to put so much focus on the look and feel of these little darlings, and yet for some reason we just *want* to. I spent hours and hours dreaming up the design of my first business card and a lot of money getting them printed. No boring rectangle for me! I was going with a unique *square* shape. Moreover, I would use metallic ink to really cement the upscale look. I thought I had cracked the code! But when I opened the box, I discovered my business cards had the exact look and feel of . . . condom wrappers. To this day I cringe at what people must have thought when I handed them out at networking events! So no matter how much fun it sounds to design them, ditch the idea of business cards. They're just procrastination in the guise of "doing business." Instead, focus on creating content— a strategy we'll discuss in depth in the chapters that follow!

- **Don't wait until you have a website.** Websites are key components of all sorts of businesses nowadays, but do not let the idea that you don't have a website keep you from making progress! The thought *But I need to create a website before I do anything else* is another very convincing excuse that keeps too many would-be business owners in their unsatisfying day jobs. You can make your exit and begin working with customers *while* also simultaneously working on building your website. It will all come together over time, and I'm going to help you create a simple and effective one in Chapter 6. Patience, grasshopper!

- **Don't allow yourself to overthink it.** It's normal to go over every single *what if* and *what about* a million times before you finally make the leap into entrepreneurship. But if you're letting these questions stall your progress, you're going to regret it. You've already made the decision. You've chosen your exit date. Heck, you've even put the date on a sticky note where you can see it daily! You *are* doing this, so get into action. Mountains get moved one small step at a time; you just have to get the ball rolling.

TELL TRUSTED FAMILY AND FRIENDS

Now that you've created your runway, it's time to tell a few supportive family members or friends. Did your heart just stop? Did your stomach flip? I know—it's scary! But something important happens when you tell people about your plan: you start to own it. I want you to stand in your decision with courage and power. I want you to make it real by telling just a few people in your life—those you know for sure will support you on this journey and keep you accountable.

Once the date was set, I told three people—and only three people. First I told my husband, Hobie, who was incredibly supportive and wanted it to happen even sooner. I had to remind him that I needed to work out a few things first (aka implement my runway) and that I wanted to have a little extra money in the bank before I left. (Spoiler alert: I did *not* end up having extra money in the bank when I left, and it still worked out.)

Next I told my mom. While not all moms are as supportive as mine, I knew my dream was safe with her. (I could tell my mom I wanted to switch careers and become the first astronaut to land on an unidentified planet and she would say, "Go for it!")

And finally, I told my dear friend Gigi. I knew she believed in me with all her heart, even when I did not believe in myself. And true to form, she held space for me when things got scary leading up to my exit.

Only three people knew my plan, and that was enough to keep me accountable—especially as the date got nearer and I started having moments of doubt. I'd ask Hobie, "Do I really need to quit my job? Maybe I could just have a side hustle indefinitely and do both." Then he'd gently remind me that I could do whatever I wanted, but that I wasn't happy in my current situation, and that my dream was to be my own boss. These moments of doubt will happen for you too—so make sure you find your people and ask them to keep you accountable to what you want most.

If I encouraged you to share your new plans with just three people, who would those people be? Do you already know? If so, wonderful. Have the conversation with each person in the next 48 hours to ensure you keep moving forward. If the thought of sharing your new plans for your future with someone in particular, let's say your partner, is stirring up something inside you, let's play a little game.

Take a minute and think about what is holding you back from sharing. What do you think they are going to say to you? Do you think they're going to tell you it's a bad idea? That you've lost your mind? Will they point out all the stops and starts you've had in your past as evidence that this is just another wild idea that's going to die out soon enough? Will they say you are not ready? Will they tell you all the reasons why you should not do it? Will they tell you that you're being reckless?

More often than not, what we fear will happen is far worse than what ultimately happens. We might be afraid to have a hard conversation, but when we finally muster up the courage to do it, we walk away thinking, *Wow. That was not nearly as hard as I thought it would be. I wish I had done it sooner.* When our expectations are outlandishly worse than reality, it's usually because we are unknowingly projecting our own fears outward—anticipating a lack of support because we don't want to fully own the decision ourselves.

Before we move forward, I want you to pause and make sure that you *own* this decision to leave your job and become your own boss, *whether or not others in your life understand or support you.* I know that's a bold request, but it's an incredibly empowering move. The truth is that people in your life may *not* support your decision. They may question you at every turn. They may say you are being irresponsible. Reckless. Irrational. And you have to be ready for it. You have to build up your armor so that the only opinion that matters is yours.

Now you might say, "Whoa, Amy. That's not true. I have a spouse and their opinion matters." It actually doesn't. I know that might sting, but stay with me here. Right now I want you to focus on what *you* need and want. If you do, you will create something that will not only bring you joy and fulfillment, but will inevitably have a positive impact for those you deeply care about as well. Your loved ones are already a part of the equation, whether they support you or not. And to help you navigate potentially difficult conversations with loved ones, I've created a script (page 255) that you can use to help you find the words that will best express your new plan and why it's important to you.

The truth is, many people just won't "get it," and that is fine. You don't have to wait for *anyone* to "get it." Plus, other people's opinions on this matter won't pay the bills. Keep moving forward with your plans, even if you don't have the support you think you need. If you are looking for permission to make your dreams happen, consider this your permission. Let's keep going. You're doing great!

We've talked about who you should tell, but let's also talk about who we will *not* be telling just yet. Let's not tell anyone who will say you're not thinking clearly. Let's not tell anyone who is always negative, who we know will recite all the reasons your plan won't work. I call these people your naysayers—and for now, they don't get to know your plans. Instead, you're only telling those people who will celebrate with you, who will support you and be your biggest cheerleaders along the way.

Of course there are people in your life that will eventually need to know, such as a spouse. If they happen to be a naysayer, hold off from sharing your plan until you're further along in developing it. That way when the time is right, you will be sharing your plans from a more confident, grounded place.

Also, some people who you chose not to tell may hear about your plans or start to question some of the changes they see you making. To ensure you stay in your power and operate like the total boss that you are, I created a second script (page 256) to address these well-meaning buzzkills—which you can tweak and make your own. It's designed to help you communicate with the naysayers in a way that protects your dreams and your heart, while staying true to yourself and respecting your own boundaries.

GIVE NOTICE

When I dialed Tony's number to give notice, my stomach was in my throat and my hands were shaky. I wasn't afraid to tell Tony as much as I was afraid that telling him meant I had to actually go through with it. *What the heck am I doing?!* was the question that played on a never-ending loop in my mind.

What got me through that experience was knowing that I had put a few pieces in place to get things going, and no matter what, I was quitting and starting my own business. The decision was made. That night I had planned a little dinner with my closest girlfriends to celebrate, so I knew I needed to make it official before we all met that evening.

When you resign, you'll likely be full of doubt—or at least lots of nerves. Sometimes we just need to stay in the moment and get it done, no matter how we are feeling, and this will certainly be one of those times. To help you navigate your resignation, here are a few guidelines to follow.

The Dos and Don'ts of Giving Notice

- *Do* plan your resignation. It's important that you find the appropriate way to quit your current situation. I want you to quit on your terms so that you feel in control and at peace with your decision. You might choose to meet with someone specifically, such as your boss or the human resources team to inform them of your resignation. You also might want to write a formal resignation letter. It would be ideal to know in advance who you feel you need to communicate with so that you have a plan. For me, I first discussed my resignation with my direct supervisor and then I called Tony to let him know. I normally would not suggest discussing your resignation with the head of the company, but out of respect—since I'd worked so closely with Tony—I felt it was necessary. Once these two key people were informed, I told my team. Ask yourself, who needs to know and in what order?

- *Do* decide your transition timeline in advance. The name of this book is *Two Weeks Notice*, and giving your current employer two weeks of notice is a gesture of goodwill and respect. That said, you may want to give more time—especially if you have been with the company for a while. But a word of caution: if you make your transition timeline too lengthy, things will likely get complicated. The longer you stay after you give notice, the easier it will be for you to feel anxious and agi-tated. After all, your new life is waiting for you to end this chapter and start the new one! I chose my exit date six months in advance, but my tran-sition after officially giving my notice was one full month, and to me that felt just right. It was enough time for me to wrap up a few smaller proj-ects, organize the details for any unfinished proj-ects, and make sure I communicated everything I needed to with team members.

My student Kenya offered her employer a three-month transition period, which she says she now regrets. Not only did the time feel as if it were dragging along, but she found herself even more stressed and in the weeds, trying to cram as much work as she could into three short months.

One more word of caution. When you offer your employer notice, it's just that—an offer. It's not a guarantee. In some cases, they'll let you know that the day you give notice will be your last day on the job—even if you're willing to stay for two weeks or longer. Just in case, I want you to be ready for your final day to be the day you resign. Let me remind you that you are stronger than you think, and no matter what happens, you will deal with it and keep moving forward. You are more capable than you know!

- **Don't share more than you are comfortable sharing.** You might be wondering how much you should tell your current employer about why you are leaving and your plans to start your own busi-ness. The answer is: it is entirely up to you. When I left Tony Robbins, I was vague—mostly because

I didn't have everything worked out and was not comfortable sharing details that were foggy at best. When people asked why I was leaving, I shared that I was going to do freelance work and help small businesses with their social media. Even though my dreams were bigger than that, it was completely true for the moment. Your employer will understandably be curious, so it's best to be prepared for them to ask you why you're leaving and where you are going next. But you do not owe them an explanation, and you can tell them as little or as much as feels good to you.

- **Don't burn bridges.** Once you resign and agree to your transition plan, go out gracefully and with no regrets. Your employer will likely need to find your replacement and you might be asked to train the person coming in after you. Be flexible when appropriate, and if your timeline allows you to train your successor, do so with a positive attitude. There's no need to burn bridges, especially when you've come this far. Finish strong so that you can close this chapter of your life feeling that you did your very best.

DO THE WORK: YOUR ACTION-BY-ACTION RUNWAY PLAN CHECKLIST

Now that you understand what is included in your runway, it's time to begin working on your plan. To support you each step of the way, I've created a checklist with important runway action items. In fact, I've created multiple checklists for you as you navigate your way through this book. (A downloadable version of all checklists can be found in the online resource hub at www.twoweeksnoticebook.com/resources.)

Right now I want you to review each of the action items in the checklist so that you understand what you need to get done. Next, choose a deadline for when you will have all the action items complete. A deadline will ensure you get this done! Next up, download and print the checklist so that you have a physical copy of it. Once you have the printout, it's time to get to work.

Each week I want you to work your way through the action items, filling in the checklists action by action as you complete each and every one of them. Throughout this book you will learn even more about many of the action items below, including dialing in your business idea and creating weekly content. I've got you every step of the way! As you work your way through this book, make sure to review this checklist often to ensure you keep it front of mind and you meet your desired deadline. (Hint: It will feel fantastic once you've worked your way through the checklist. Commit to getting it done and then celebrate this milestone!)

- **Declare Your Exit Date**
  My exit date will be

  _____

- **Research the Appropriate Way to Resign**
  Who will you meet with specifically?

  _____

  Do you need to write a formal resignation letter? If so, to whom?

  _____

- **Brainstorm Your "You" Factor (Check out Chapter 4 for extra support)**

   Briefly describe your online business starter idea below:

   _____

   _____

   _____

   _____

   _____

   _____

- **Create Your Financial Plan**

   Briefly describe your temporary financial plan below:

   _____

   _____

   _____

   _____

   _____

   _____

   _____

- **Create Your First Piece of Content and Post It**
  Content topic:

  _____

  _____

  _____

  _____

  _____

  _____

  _____

  Will it be audio, video, or written?

  _____

  _____

  _____

  Where will you post it?

  _____

  _____

  _____

  _____

  _____

- **Create New Home Work Space or Secure Co-Working Space**
  Where will you work?

  _____

  _____

  _____

  _____

  _____

  _____

  _____

- **Share Plans with a Few Supportive Family Members/Friends**
  Who will you tell and why?

  _____

  _____

  _____

  _____

  _____

  _____

  _____

Chapter 3

Getting Down to Business
How to Set Yourself Up for Success

One afternoon when I was still at my corporate job, I found myself crammed under my desk, in the fetal position, whispering into the phone. If anyone had walked in at that very moment, my peculiar behavior would have raised some red flags, to say the least! But the walls in my office were thin, and I was talking with a woman who had built a successful online business, very similar to the one I wanted to create. I had paid her for an hour-long consultation so I could ask a million and one questions about how she had done it. Looking back now, hiding under the desk feels ridiculous. But at the time? Totally necessary.

That call changed everything for me. I was able to learn from someone who had gone before me. I asked her how she got started, what she did in her early days of getting her business off the ground, how she first started to make money, and what she did to grow the business. I wanted to know every detail because I didn't have a clue where to start.

Lucky for you, there will be no covert under-the-desk calls needed as you suss out your business strategy. Because now that you've decided to leave your job, and you're planning your exit date and runway, I'm taking you straight into everything you need to know to get your business off the ground. There will be no guessing and no feeling your way through the dark for you! If you follow the road map I'm laying out for you, you're sure to get started faster and more efficiently than 99 percent of those who venture out to start their businesses. Including me!

Speaking of which, the first thing I learned (the hard way) when I went out on my own was that working for myself was not the same as working in an office, under the oversight of a supervisor, with a department of people working all around me. (More people are working from home nowadays, so maybe you feel me on this one!) What I noticed is that without someone directing my workflow, I had no sense of appropriate *boundaries*; I didn't always know *what* to be working on; I didn't always do a good job of *protecting* my time; I didn't have a set *work space* I could always fall back on; and I didn't have anyone holding me accountable for the projects I wanted to complete. I had to come up with my own habits for each of these key areas, and when I did, the work really started to click. So as you start getting to work on your own, let's go through each of these important areas—so you don't have to stumble and fall the way I did!

SETTING YOUR NON-NEGOTIABLES

One of the most important lessons I've learned after more than a decade in business is that if you don't set boundaries, both personal and professional, you'll be pulled in way too many directions—causing you to feel overwhelmed and lost—and you'll easily lose sight of your why (aka the reason you're working so dang hard to make it all happen!). Trust me when I say that I am speaking from personal experience here, which includes years of burnout and resentment. I learned the hard way that when you don't set and keep parameters around your work life, your dreams, goals, and desires are at risk.

In the first few years of building my business, I overcommitted out of anxiety. I wanted to make sure it thrived, and so I ended up saying yes to just about everything that came my way. Like so many entrepreneurs just starting out, I didn't have enough experience yet to know what was a good use of time—and what definitely *wasn't*. I succumbed to unnecessary distractions and allowed my business life to creep into my personal life. Let me be clear: some work-life creep is perfectly normal and hard to avoid. (How can you tell whether a networking event is a good use of your time unless you go once and see?) But as I saw in my own experience and that of too many of my students, overcommitment can become an addiction. We can start to believe that if we're not working 24/7, we're not doing *enough*.

To help you head burnout off at the pass, I want you to create an actual list of what I call your non-negotiables. These are the boundaries that follow your values and goals, clearly defining what you will and will not allow in your personal and professional life. A good non-negotiable is personal, specific, and clearly tied to what is most important to you. For example, you may be a mom whose reason for giving notice and starting a business is to be home every afternoon when your kids get off the bus from school. So you might set a non-negotiable that says you do not schedule work meetings after 3 P.M., regardless of how important it seems to be.

You might be asking, "How do I know which non-negotiables are a good fit for me?" and my answer is to simply pay attention to where you're struggling. I know you're thinking, *Geez, that sounds fun!* But truly, continual frustration, overwhelm, resentment, and generalized unhappiness are your allies here. See them as your guides in this process. They shine a light on what's not working for you right now so that you can address each of those struggles with a solution—aka a non-negotiable.

For example, let's say you're feeling overwhelmed and stressed out as you get your business up and running. One of your non-negotiables might be that you add two hours of "self-care time" into your schedule each week to give yourself the opportunity for a much-needed mental health break. This one promise to yourself could dramatically change how you feel and show up when you dive back into your work.

To help you define your own non-negotiables, I'm going to share three that I live by myself, just to get your own ideas flowing. These have been total game-changers in my life—and I think they'll resonate with you too. They are: *Hobie Is My Priority, Working Hours Exist*, and *Social Media Will Not Own Me*. Let's dive into each one.

Non-negotiable #1: Hobie Is My Priority

At one point Hobie and I were constantly arguing about "how much time I was working," which really meant "how little time I was spending with him." The same conversation was on a constant loop and caused a lot of friction in our house. My relationship with Hobie is the single most important relationship in my life, so I knew I needed to do something different.

I sat down one afternoon and journaled about the important areas in both my personal and professional lives that were causing me pain. I wrote about the constant arguments and my subsequent resentment toward Hobie for telling me I worked too much. I wrote about how

I felt I couldn't come up for air because there was just too much to get done. I was mad. Mad at the work in front of me, mad at Hobie, mad at myself. About 20 minutes into my journaling, my writing hand was throbbing and tears were streaming down my face as I looked down to see the last thing I wrote. *I miss my husband.*

At that moment, I created my non-negotiable list. Non-negotiable number one: *Hobie is my priority.* To make this one stick, I had to allow *No* (or *No, but thanks for asking*) to be a complete sentence. I couldn't say yes to everything that was coming my way, or I'd be working 70-hour weeks. I won't say it was easy, as the recovering people pleaser I am. I hate disappointing people. But keeping my top priority in my line of vision—time with Hobie and a strong and successful marriage—gave me the confidence to say no.

Non-negotiable #2: Working Hours Exist

My second non-negotiable is to set working hours—and stick to them. (Listen, I never said your non-negotiables would be easy to implement, but I can promise you it will be 100 percent worth it if you do!) I'm embarrassed to admit this, but I have the type of personality where I could work 15 hours a day. It helps that I love what I get to do, but working 15 hours a day is not healthy for anyone—and it's a surefire way to burn out. So for my non-negotiable number two, I wanted to be super clear about the time I committed to working—and the time I committed to stepping away from work and taking care of my personal life.

The line between "work time" and "time off" can be very, very blurry, especially for those of us who work from home. I firmly believe that the idea of "work-life balance"—at least the 50/50 type—does not exist. However, work-life *integration* is possible. The key is to be intentional about it.

If you're anything like me, then you know it's easy to make work a priority. But I wanted to make my personal life a priority too—my health, my self-care, and my loved ones.

Even though it was terrifying, I began to intentionally schedule periods during my day when I wouldn't work—and block that time in my calendar so I was sure I'd take it. I started to block time off before work to start my morning with journaling, coffee with Hobie, and walking my dog, Scout. I also started to block time for lunch every day. To my surprise, I discovered that Parkinson's law—the adage that work expands to fill the time available for its completion—was really true. Even though I kept fewer working hours, I got just as much done, if not more!

For you, work-life integration might mean working six-hour days instead of eight-hour days. Maybe you'll commit to having a no-work zone after 7 P.M., or perhaps you'll decide that you never start your day until 10 A.M. Whatever works for you and supports the kind of lifestyle you want to be living is perfect.

Non-negotiable #3: Social Media Will Not Own Me

My third and final non-negotiable was to limit my intake of social media. This one was tough! I found myself mindlessly scrolling through Instagram, only to come up for air an hour later and be amazed I'd just lost so much time. I'm sure you've been there, the "let me just check one thing real quick," becomes 45 minutes of scrolling, scrolling, scrolling. Meanwhile, there's an important person in the same room that you're not spending quality time with or an important task in your business that could have been checked off. I lost count of how many times Hobie would kindly ask, "What are you looking at?" and I'd realize I'd been scrolling through social media looking at . . . nothing. It was like I was in a trance. He lovingly pulled me out of it, but I didn't want him to have to. I wanted to use my time well, and mindlessly consuming social media did not make the list.

If I wanted to make big strides in my business while still having time for my family, I knew I needed to limit these scrolling sessions. I made a commitment to not look at social media during my morning routine, made a "no phones" rule for family time, and gave myself a daily scrolling allotment. My team and I also have a distraction-free rule for meetings, which means we silence our phones, put them out of reach, and turn off notifications. This way we're all focused and present while we're together. Yes, I definitely slip occasionally and find myself texting during a meeting or scrolling on Instagram when I'm with Hobie, but ever since I declared my intentions, these little slipups have been few and far between.

I set these boundaries because I knew I was missing out on the experiences happening right in front of me. Time is too precious, and I didn't want to waste it anymore.

DO THE WORK: YOUR NON-NEGOTIABLES

Now I want you to think about setting up your own non-negotiables. Remember, if you do this, you will protect your calendar, your focus and productivity, your mindset, and your relationships. All of which are so very important for you to create the business and life of your dreams. The key to success here is to commit to sticking to them.

> **Step 1:** Find a cozy spot and grab your journal. I want you to take just 10 minutes to write a list of the current challenges that keep coming up for you. What are some daily habits that you are doing that no longer support your future goals? What's keeping

you stuck? What is making you feel resentful? Are you doing something regularly that is getting in the way of your happiness and success? What are some distractions that you know are slowing you down? Take this time to journal your thoughts or just write a simple list. The important thing here is to get it out of your head and onto paper.

Step 2: Go back to your list and review what you wrote down. Which challenges stand out to you the most? Circle the top three.

Step 3: Create a non-negotiable for each of your top three. When you craft them, think about your values and your goals. What are you working toward? What is most important to you? From there, ask yourself, what boundary, habit, or behavior can you commit to consistently to help you move closer to what is most important?

To help you create your non-negotiables, here is a list of common boundaries to spark your inspiration:

- No working on weekends

- Stop working at 5 P.M. each day

- Get at least eight hours of sleep each night

- Move your body for at least 30 minutes each day

- Make time for a 20-minute nap each afternoon

- Only say yes when you mean it

- Always make time for school pickup

- No screens at the dinner table

THE TIGER TIME RITUAL

As you start turning your attention—and your time—toward your own business, you may bump up against a feeling that there is not enough time to do everything required to get your runway built. Not enough time to create that website, not enough time to post as much as you want to on social media, not enough time to fulfill the orders you've received, not enough time to respond to all the emails. The fact is, feeling like there's not enough time means only one thing: you have arrived! Welcome to the real world of entrepreneurship.

As you build your runway, I assure you life will just seem to get busier. Your current job, kids, pets, appointments—you name it—will be there, pulling your attention away from the steps you need to get your business off the ground. Since your dreams and goals are on the line like never before, it's critical to develop a time-management system that protects your time for the actions that will drive your business forward—even when the rest of your responsibilities are clamoring for your attention.

Introducing Tiger Time!

Tiger Time is the part of your day that you fiercely protect (like a tiger with her cub!) to give yourself dedicated space to focus on the areas that matter most for your business right now. The rules are strict, but the rewards are huge.

For me, Tiger Time has always been about content creation. As you'll see in Chapter 7, I am incredibly dedicated to creating content to support my community and the business. But being creative takes time, energy, and focus, and making space for it did not come easy. My mind would be telling me about the million other things that were more important than writing the worksheet for next week's podcast episode. But ever since I started implementing Tiger Time, I've seen incredible results.

My podcast has grown exponentially since I began producing it consistently, to the tune of over 50 million downloads and counting. My social media engagement has skyrocketed since I committed to posting regularly, meaning my audience can depend on hearing from me on a daily basis. I credit these huge leaps to Tiger Time.

Now I want you to create a Tiger Time ritual of your very own. Here's how it's going to work. For the next 30 days, I want you to decide *when* and for *how long* you are going to work on your business—choosing which days of the week you'll schedule Tiger Time and the length of time you'll commit for each session.

For example, let's say you are going to commit to working on your business on Tuesday and Thursday mornings and on Saturdays. Once you choose your days, you'll choose your times. Let's say you decide to work from 7 to 9 A.M. on Tuesdays and Thursdays and from 12 to 3 P.M. on Saturdays. The most important step happens next: schedule it to make it real. That means you'll go into your calendar and block out the time. Label it "Tiger Time" to remind yourself that this appointment is precious, and you want to be fierce with keeping your commitment.

Warning: As Tiger Time comes up in your schedule, you're going to be tempted to skip it. You'll want to use this time for something more urgent that's happening in your life. When we're working on a new business, it feels new and uncertain. As a result, when we dip into the work, it can feel uncomfortable and awkward, and we can become full of doubt. What happens next? We come up with very effective strategies to hide from the discomfort—namely making everything else more urgent or important.

I can't stress this enough: unless you see this pattern for what it is—fear of the unknown—you can end up with *years* flying by and no progress being made. Don't let this be you! If you commit to Tiger Time, staying with the feelings and allowing yourself to be uncomfortable, I promise this too shall pass. Soon you'll find yourself working on your business with focus and flow. The alternative is that you end up putting off your dreams—and that's just not going to do!

I want you to take a moment to imagine what will happen in your business if you stick to your Tiger Time schedule. Imagine the momentum and clarity that will come with this commitment. Imagine how much trust and self-confidence you'll build in yourself, as you keep your word over and over. Pretty great, right?

Now, I want you to imagine what will happen if you *don't* make time for your business. If you let the Tiger Time in your calendar slip by, telling yourself there are other more important things for you to be doing. In her book *Year of Yes*, the hugely successful television producer Shonda Rhimes quotes the commencement speech she gave at her alma mater Dartmouth two years before: "Dreams are lovely. But they are just dreams. Fleeting, ephemeral, pretty. But dreams do not come true just because you dream them. It's hard work that makes things happen. It's hard work that creates change."

At first it might feel like a huge inconvenience to make room for Tiger Time, but Steve Jobs said it best: "Focus and simplicity . . . Once you get there, you can move mountains." I couldn't agree more. The business that you are growing deserves your focus, time, and attention. It's up to you to create the space to make that happen.

CREATING AND PROTECTING YOUR WORK SPACE

If you can't tell by now, I really want to help you protect and optimize your time so you can start to build your business with certainty. But there's another component to work-from-home success that I want you to take equally seriously: the space you'll be working in. After 14 years of working at home, I've become a pro at creating a work space that allows for both creativity and productivity. Since it's much more common to work from home these days, you might already have your setup dialed in. But if you're new to the work-from-home life—or you'd just welcome some new tips—here are my top pieces of advice for creating an optimized WFH experience:

- **Set up a designated "work space" if you don't already have one.** The key is to find a space in your home that is quiet and distraction-free. (Or at least as low-distraction as possible!) It's ideal if this space will be used solely as your work space versus it also moonlighting as a family space. For example, choosing your kitchen table is not the best choice if you can help it, because you'll be interrupted by your family coming in and out of the kitchen and you'll have to move your work for mealtimes. Also, although it's not always possible, try to find a space that has a door, giving yourself as much privacy as possible.

- **Make your space distraction-free.** I'm talking both about physical distraction and *emotional* distraction. Do you need to turn your phone and all other notifications off? Do you need to put a do-not-disturb sign on your door? Do you need to share with your family when you will be working so that they can respect your work time? You're going to need to be intentional about this because it's not going to happen on its own!

- **Set the mood.** What do you need to add to make it a more *creative* space? Do you need to clear the clutter off your desk each day before you get started? Would lighting a candle, playing soft focus music, or turning on a white-noise machine help you concentrate during your session? Think about the times in your life you've been the most focused and what the physical space was like. Try to bring some similar elements into your work space if you can.

- **Consider a co-working space.** If you look around your house and realize there is just no space for you to work—or if you're one of those people who concentrates better when there are other people around—consider investing in a co-working space. I've done this in the past when my home life was especially chaotic, and it was a lifesaver. You can rent a small space on a monthly basis, or you can pay even less and use the desks provided in the common areas. Co-working spaces are often quiet and set up in a way that encourages focus and efficiency. Plus, they offer networking opportunities.

The most important thing to remember is that you get to decide when you work, how you work, and where you work. Owning and running an online business means you can essentially work from wherever you choose. Lifestyle and location freedom are two of the biggest perks of being your own boss!

GET AN ACCOUNTABILITY PARTNER

About two years into starting my business, I realized I didn't love the business I had started. I was doing a lot of consulting and working with individual coaching clients, but I didn't enjoy the work. I desperately wanted to change my business model, but I didn't know how I was going to do it. I was a mess. During that time, I didn't have anyone to ask questions to or seek advice from. I was lonely and tired and felt like things would never go my way.

If only I'd had a trusted friend to call or text—someone who understood exactly what I was going through—I'm sure those months would have been much more bearable. Plus, I might even have received advice that would have allowed me to make some much-needed pivots in my business. Instead I floundered for months until I had the courage to shift my business model to selling online digital courses, which proved to be my sweet spot. However, looking back, I know that I could have sidestepped so much confusion and overwhelm if I had reached out to a peer for support. Moral of the story? Don't ever go at it alone. Find someone you can check in with, and do it often. This person is what I call an *accountability partner*.

My student C.Lee, a Certified Professional Organizer, found a small group of accountability partners right from the start. When she created her first online training program all about how to get organized, she was also dealing with taking care of her much older sick sister, which added immense stress to her already-full plate. But her loyal "podsisters" were by her side as she created and launched her program, encouraging her to keep going. They still meet every Sunday to support and encourage each other, and C.Lee attributes her $16,000 first launch success in part to these supportive women who bolstered her and offered guidance each step of the way.

I believe everyone needs an accountability partner or group, and I myself have had several. Some I paid to help me stay accountable, and some have been dear friends. The best partners I've had are other entrepreneurs, in the same industry as me. Why? Because they understand me, my business, and why I work so hard. No matter who you choose, your accountability partner must "get" you and what you're doing. That way they can support you in a personalized, relevant way.

When I first left my corporate job, I joined a paid mastermind that was uncomfortably expensive. I did not tell a soul (except Hobie) that I was joining, because no one in my life at the time would have understood why I would have paid that kind of money. But at the time, it was the only way I knew how to insert myself into a group of women who were in the trenches like me, building businesses online and juggling busy lives. I was driven by the group's energy, and women in the group were checking in with me regularly, making sure I was moving toward the goals I had set for myself.

Although I loved my pricey mastermind, you don't have to pay an arm and a leg for an incredible accountability partner. I've had other equally powerful accountability experiences with no price tag attached. I personally put together an accountability group of entrepreneurial women who were all peers of mine, and we started a text group to check in with each other for a full year.

No fees were involved and the rules were clear: We would text each other when we had questions about things like marketing funnels, copywriting, hiring, and firing. We would share with the group when we were in a funk and ask for advice on how to get out of it. We would share our wins and losses and everything in between. In addition to our group texts, we would meet on Zoom once a quarter and each of us would take a hot seat, where we would share what was working and not working, getting insight and support from the group. We ended each Zoom by setting individual goals for the coming quarter.

Today I keep myself accountable by checking in with just one specific girlfriend, almost daily via text. I tell her what I am working on, and then she shares what she is working on. When we get stuck or have questions, we reach out to one another. There are no formal rules, and it feels very organic but also incredibly powerful.

Now think about it: As you venture out into your new life and business, who in your life would be a good candidate for an accountability partner? What friend, small group, or supportive family member can you ask to check in with you to ensure you are showing up for your business, staying focused, and keeping your commitments to yourself? The key here is that you need to go out and find your accountability partners; don't wait for them to find you. Be proactive with your pursuit now so that you'll have the support in place when you need it.

Before we dive deeper into exactly what work you're going to be accountable *for*, let's have a little pep talk. I can't take the credit for this one, because it's the exact same pep talk Hobie gave me many years ago at a particularly tough time in my journey.

I was about one year into starting my own business, working on my first digital course launch and feeling a bit overwhelmed and unsure of my abilities. I looked at him, tears welling up in my eyes.

"This is too hard," I said. "I feel like a hot mess most days. I am literally making this up as I go, and I am not even sure if what I am doing is right!"

Hobie looked at me. "You will never have all the answers. You can't wait until you have your business all figured out, because that day will never come." He reminded me that there would always be more to learn, more to know, more to do.

"Snooks," he said—embarrassingly, that's what he's always called me—"you don't need anything more than what you have right now; you just need to get started. You won't always get it right, so don't beat yourself up. As long as you never give up, you will succeed. Let me believe in you until you're ready to believe in yourself. You can do this!"

When he was done, I dried my eyes and got back to work. If you don't have a Hobie in your life to give you this same sort of pep talk right now, that's okay. Because *I* am giving it to you right now.

I'm standing in front of you, speaking from my heart. *You can do this. You're amazing for even getting started. I believe in you completely.* And please know, my friend, that it's true.

Chapter 4

Dial In Your "You" Factor
How to Define Your Business Topic

Let's pick up where we left off in that San Diego conference room 14 years ago. As I was sitting around that table, listening to all these stories of success, I knew I wanted more. I wanted to start calling the shots and to create a business by my own design.

In an effort to hold myself accountable to this dream, I shared my ambitions with a friend in my office. She was very receptive and encouraging. But when she asked, "What type of business do you want to start?" I stared at her like a deer in the headlights. It's not just that I didn't have a "big idea"; I didn't have the *first clue* what kind of offer I could make that people would actually want to buy.

This friend regularly wrote speaking presentation outlines and training materials like digital products and workbook guides. I remember thinking, *She's so lucky. She could be a writer if she wanted to. She has* something. *I have nothing.*

I felt like I had none of what I now call the "you" factor—a clear understanding of the unique product or service that only I could bring to the world. Back when I was a kid and adults would ask about my professional aspirations—which, in an American childhood, happens every five seconds—I was always at a loss. *How does anybody know what they want to be when they grow up?* I would think.

But the questions kept coming, so one day I asked my mom what *she* thought I should do. Without hesitation, she suggested I become a flight attendant. From that point onward, when my adult relatives would ask me, "Amy, what do you want to be when you grow up?" I would proudly reply, "A flight attendant!" Which sounded like a reasonable choice, except for one small detail: I truly had zero idea what a flight attendant did.

Later in a high school creative writing class, we were given an assignment titled "Jobs I'd Like to Have," and I researched what a flight attendant actually did. The discovery made me queasy—literally. I've always gotten intensely motion sick; flying for a living sounded like my own personal hell. When I asked my mom why she chose that profession for me, she replied, "I always wished I had traveled more and seen more of the world. So I wanted that for you." All this time I had been playing out my mom's dream, not mine!

Now here I was, a dozen years later, wanting so much to take the leap into starting my own business—and still having no idea what I wanted to be when I grew up! In the meantime, Tony was preparing to launch an online marketing campaign to promote his latest digital course.

Funnily enough, the course was about creating a life on your own terms. And as luck would have it, getting to work on this project gave me the opportunity to get a crash course in online marketing: websites, lead generation, funnels, webinars, launches, and so much more. I found myself truly enjoying everything I was learning.

I'd also seen all the different ways individuals were taking that kind of knowledge and turning it into full-time consulting work. Suddenly I put two and two together: those men I'd heard talking about "lifestyle freedom" were talking about what it felt like to run their own businesses, and it was online marketing that had given them that opportunity.

Online marketing—the exact thing I'm learning right now! I realized the knowledge I was accumulating could be of *so much help* to other entrepreneurs trying to build online businesses and create digital courses. With that, the seed of my future was planted.

YOUR NORTH STAR: DETERMINING YOUR "YOU" FACTOR

The journey I took to flesh out my "big idea" was filled with speed bumps, potholes, and too many missteps to count. But once you find that idea—the "you" factor that sets you and your business apart—everything, and I mean *everything*, comes into focus. Business by its nature is still filled with obstacles and challenges, but you have a north star to guide you along your way. Once I knew that I wanted to help other entrepreneurs build online businesses and create digital courses, I had more clarity and purpose moving forward inside my business.

My goal in this chapter is to help you start determining the "you" factor that will make your online business stand out from the crowd. Do you get compliments on how you put your outfits together or how organized your closet is? Have you mastered the art of family dinners in under 30 minutes? Do your co-workers often ask you for help with technology or a specific software? Are you the one your friends come to for craft ideas? Have you figured out how to grow an engaged following on social media?

In Chapters 11 and 12, I'm going to walk you through three revenue-generating business models I've used in my own business throughout the years. But I want to give you a snapshot of each model here, so you can keep them in mind as you read through the exercises in this chapter— and as you start determining your "you" factor.

Revenue Strategy #1:
Coaching or Consulting Sessions

Whether these are one-on-one coaching sessions, group coaching sessions, or consulting sessions, this is a great business model if you have specific knowledge and you already have (or can easily create) a system for teaching or guiding others on what you know.

Revenue Strategy #2:
Service-Based Work

This model involves taking your "you" factor and applying it in real life by offering your customers a service they really need. Different from coaching or consulting—where you teach your customers how to do something themselves—a service-based business provides that actual service *for* them. For example, a CPA who does your taxes or web developer who manages your website.

Revenue Strategy #3:
Build a Workshop Course

Create an online one-hour training that gives your audience a quick win and addresses an immediate need or challenge they are facing.

If you're daydreaming about becoming your own boss but simultaneously beating yourself up or feeling unworthy because you don't have a world-changing idea, remember this. When I encountered online marketing, I discovered something I was good at, that could help other people, and that I enjoyed. It wasn't going to save the world, and that's okay! Not every business has to cure a disease or solve world hunger—in fact, most don't. But it was really *me*—and that's what matters. Don't stop yourself before you even start by placing unnecessary standards on the talents and value you bring to the table.

You could be like Alisha, who created a program helping parents with picky eaters and provided enough financial freedom for her husband to be able to retire. Or Natalie, who took her experience as a sommelier and turned it into an online course helping others buy, taste, and pair wine like an expert, enrolling more than 100 students in her beta launches. Or Karida, who teaches instructors how to deliver tap dance classes that excite students and increase class enrollments—and now feels like her life has purpose, since she impacts not only her own students but *their* students as well.

These ideas may not lead to Nobel Peace Prizes, but they've led to more freedom, joy, family time, money, and satisfaction than Alisha, Natalie, or Karida could have imagined. The ideas certainly made an impact in these women's lives and those of their students. And there's nothing wrong with that.

DO THE WORK: WHAT DO YOU REALLY WANT?

When you think of your big idea for your business, I want it to light you up. This simple exercise is meant to help you wander into the depths of your wildest dreams to find out what you'd *really* love to do.

1. Find a quiet spot, bring a journal or tablet to write on, and make sure you can be seated comfortably and undisturbed for about 10 minutes. Set a timer if that helps you, or just commit to doing the exercise until it comes to its natural completion.

2. Close your eyes and take a few deep breaths. Then remind yourself this exercise is not about

censoring, editing, or criticizing yourself. It's not about being reasonable or rational. This exercise is about accessing your own truest desire, which is usually found buried under a lot of rules. Let go of the rules. In this exercise, no idea is a bad idea. We're just letting our thoughts unfold organically. No one ever has to know the things that come up; this is just for you.

3. Once you're ready, ask yourself the following question: *If I couldn't fail, and money wasn't an issue, what would I want to do for a living?* Let the question repeat itself over and over in your mind as your answers unfold.

4. Take notes in your journal as you go or hold them to write down at the end. Every answer is valuable and worthy—there is no right or wrong way to do this exercise.

You may come up with your big idea or you may not. The goal is to give your imagination the freedom to generate ideas, to start to see what's possible, and to let go of the limiting beliefs you have around what you can and can't do. You are capable of so much more than you give yourself credit for. You just have to be willing to dream a little—and put in the work.

THE SWEET SPOT

To help you develop the idea for your business and an understanding of what sets that idea—and ultimately you—apart, I offer you what I call "the sweet spot test." A business idea passes this test, and thus becomes a viable option for your next venture when it represents the intersection of these four things:

1. Your 10 percent edge

2. A struggle, challenge, desire, or need you see in the world

3. Your profit potential

4. A topic that truly lights you up

Your 10 Percent Edge

Often people feel like they have to be the "expert of all experts" when starting a business, but the truth is, you don't. You don't need an advanced degree to prove that you are an authority in the field. You don't need to be an acclaimed author, and you don't need to have a million followers. You only need a 10 percent edge—that means being just 10 percent ahead of your students' knowledge and ability.

We *all* have skills, and that includes you. Your 10 percent edge represents what you *already* have experience doing—the knowledge you've accumulated or the transformation you've either achieved for yourself or helped others achieve. Have you created a unique system to use? Do you have a specific way of doing something that can be replicated? Are you sharing a new approach to an existing topic?

Let me give you an example. One of my students, Scarlett, was in the market for a new job and began documenting her job search on YouTube. Soon she had generated $5,000 in ad revenue and attracted 20,000 subscribers.

Scarlett took it as a sign: it was time to turn her hobby into a true side hustle. She took what she had learned about making money with videos and created a digital course, YouTube Made Simple, teaching others how to do what she'd done. Scarlett wasn't a YouTube expert, but she'd had success making money with the platform. Soon she was able to use the profits generated from her course to start a business that now generates six figures annually. She took her 10 percent edge and made it work for her in a big way.

Think about what everyone is *always* asking you about. What brings your friends, family, and colleagues to you for advice? What could you talk about all day and never get bored? Something you think seems "too simple" or is second nature to you might feel completely unattainable to someone else. If you're just a little bit ahead of your audience and you've gotten results for yourself or someone else, you have exactly what it takes to be a successful entrepreneur.

A Struggle, Challenge, Desire, or Need You See in the World

Whatever your business offers must be important enough that someone else will be willing to put skin in the game in the form of money, time, energy, and effort to see results. Does your business offer something that will make someone's life easier, providing a shortcut to solving a previously insurmountable problem or transformation they deeply want? Does your business create an opportunity for someone, giving them access to a product or service that makes their life better? Identifying this will be useful in both how you add value and how you market your product or service to the world.

Profit Potential

The next area is all about making sure your idea is financially viable. When choosing your product or service, you want to make sure it's something people will pay for. And the easiest way to do that is by paying attention to what people are *already* paying for. What type of content, products, or services does the person you're hoping to help buy? Do they buy courses, coaching, software, or apps on the topic you're considering?

Do a quick Google or Amazon search for books on your idea. Which books are the most popular and have the best reviews? What do people love about them? Are there popular podcasts on the topic? What do their reviews say? What are people raving about on social media? What are they talking about in communities and groups? A little time spent researching your idea to make sure there's truly a market for it could save you a *lot* of heartache later. In the next chapter, we'll talk more about how to validate your idea by talking directly with the people you want to serve.

What Lights You Up

Finally, your idea needs to be something you *enjoy doing*. When you love what you're doing, your excitement will show up not only in the quality of your product or service but in how you talk about it, market it, and how you show up every day. When you're working on something you don't love and things get tough, you'll want to just throw in the towel. But when it's something that inspires you, you'll feel resilient. No matter how hard it gets—when the technology fails, you get bad feedback from a customer, or a new idea you had falls flat—you'll see it as a minor setback at most. You'll be willing to do whatever it takes to make the business work, because you love it that much.

As I said earlier, what lights you up does *not* need to be your life's mission. If it is, that's incredible and I'm thrilled for you. But it doesn't need to be in order for you to be successful. Your business just needs to be an enthusiastic *yes* for you, because this will ensure there's enough energy behind it to pull you through the tough times. The *yes* could come from a passion for the content you're sharing, the fact that teaching it is fun for you, or even just because it allows you to be there when your kids get home from school. What lights us up is totally individual—whatever floats your particular boat, as they say!

* * *

When your idea hits all four of these areas, you can feel assured you've hit your sweet spot, and that your business has that "you" factor. Take my student Andrea, for example. As a mother of five kids under eight years old who were all potty trained by the time they were walking, Andrea knew she had something special to share with other parents. Thanks to a technique she'd mastered called Elimination Communication, she certainly had the skills and know-how.

When she started talking about it with other moms in her yoga classes, she saw that there was a need and desire in the world from other parents *and* that they were willing to pay for it. And even though she never set out to create an entire business teaching others about baby potty training, after struggling to find simple solutions as a new mom, she knew that helping other parents in the same position was her true calling. She had found her sweet spot—one that now allows her to work only three hours a day, with a seven-figure business!

Now that you know how to measure the effectiveness of your business idea, I want to tackle head-on one of the biggest objections I see when students are coming up with their topic: the fear that their idea has been "done before."

NO IDEA IS ORIGINAL

When my student Niki decided to shift her business to start helping families with children experiencing stress, anxiety, or depression get the support and tools they need for their children to thrive, she thought she'd struck upon the most original idea in the world. Then she started doing research on what her audience was already paying for and *wham!* She realized there were already online trainings on this topic.

But after growing up in an abusive home and becoming a mother herself, Niki knew she had unique experiences that only she could share. Sick of playing small her whole life, she was determined to help other families stop the generational cycles and start raising confident and empowered children. So she set aside the fear that her calling "had been done before" and fearlessly put herself out there—establishing her own niche and business and offering coaching, workshops, and free resources for other families in need.

Whether you already have an idea or you've started to do some research on possible topics, you've probably noticed that there are other people already doing something similar to what you're hoping to do. And I bet an all-too-familiar voice inside shouted, *I knew it! That seat's already taken. Don't embarrass yourself. There's no room for you.*

When I first came on the scene, I wanted to teach social media to small businesses. But it turned out, so did everyone else—and their brother. It was an incredibly crowded space, and there were a few brands that had already cornered the market, so I felt like there was no room for me.

Everyone who has ever tried something new faces this feeling. In part because the fear is not entirely unfounded: there *are* hundreds of dog trainers, stylists, wellness coaches, teachers, food bloggers, and Internet marketers out there. But none of them does *exactly* what you do, the way that *you* do it. Even Mark Twain said, "There is no such thing as a new idea. It is impossible. We simply take a lot of old ideas and put them into a sort of mental kaleidoscope. We give them a turn and they make new and curious combinations."

All you have to do is identify your sweet spot and own your own unique approach to the topic you're choosing—the new and curious combination that is yours alone—then commit to a head-down drive toward the winner's circle.

The challenge with comparing yourself to everyone else is that you will rarely stack up. In our own minds, we almost always come up short. We have this magical way of deleting the long track record of accomplishments in our wake, focusing only on our fears and failures. We look around and convince ourselves that we are not far enough along or that we don't have what it takes to make our dreams real. How do we get around this little flaw of the human mind?

I want you to take a page out of Seabiscuit's playbook. Yes, I'm talking about the underdog racehorse. His secret to success? *Blinders.* Those strange-looking goggles that racehorses wear were designed to keep their focus locked on the goal in front of them rather than being distracted by all the shiny objects and competitors in the periphery. The horse can't look left and it can't look right, only forward.

My advice to you? Be a racehorse. Head down, blinders on, stay in your lane, keep going. You've got too much important work to do to be paying attention to the horses around you. Frankly, they are none of your business. Your business is right in front of you. Stay focused.

While you're at it, adopt this mantra: "There is an abundance of success to go around and I am absolutely deserving and open to receiving my share." Repeat the mantra as often as needed. When you shift your mindset from looking for all the reasons it won't work to truly believing that you not only can achieve success, but *deserve* to, the way you show up and go after your dreams will change dramatically.

FOUR EXERCISES FOR FINDING YOUR "YOU" FACTOR

Now that we've proactively addressed an objection that might come up in this next section, it's time to identify your greatest strengths—what it is that *only you* do best—and align them with what you enjoy doing *most*. Doing these four exercises will set you up to brainstorm what's unique about your particular process and how you can translate that into a product or service that can be monetized.

Exercise #1:
3 Days of No-Judgment Inspiration

Since you picked up this book, you've likely had flashes of ideas for an online business. You might've been deep in a project at work and thought, *This is something I could teach other people.* Or maybe you've seen clients or friends continue to get stuck in the same specific way over and over again, and you know you could ease their pain if you could just teach them what you know. Those are all inspirations, and you don't want to ignore them.

For the next three days, I want you to write down *every single* idea you have for your business. Feasible or not, exciting to you or not. If you have an idea for a business, it goes on the list. While I love using a journal for all things, I want you to be 100 percent sure you can capture your ideas on the fly, so my suggestion is to keep the list on your phone, in the note-taking app of your choice.

In addition, I want you to deliberately create some space to brainstorm each day. Ten minutes is plenty of time. Sit down and do a "brain dump" of every idea that pops into your head. (Feel free to use the same app or an actual pen and paper.) Don't judge your ideas as they come; editing tends to block the flow of creativity. Just write down every idea—the good, the bad, and the ugly. You'll be using this list in the "Do the Work" exercise later in the chapter.

Exercise #2:
Identify What's Already Working

When you're looking for ideas, it helps to pull inspiration from things that have already proven to be successful. Maybe you help small businesses with their taxes, or your friends come to you for help throwing parties, or you've created a simple system for planting a vegetable garden within a small space, or you have a special way to teach someone to play an instrument without reading music. Let's take a look at the areas that are already yielding the biggest results for you. Ask yourself the following questions:

- In what areas are you already being paid for your time and expertise?

- What do your friends and family come to you for advice or guidance about?

- If you have one-on-one clients, or even if you've done something successfully for yourself, what process or framework did you use to get results?

- What kind of questions do you get asked all the time? What topic are you always talking about or being asked by others to "pick your brain" about?

- What successful businesses are out there that you know you could do really well in your own unique way?

- If you already have an audience, what are the common questions or comments that come up? Which content was shared the most?

Exercise #3:
Examine Your Own Transformation

Think about all your big life experiences. Then think about where you've made yourself better along the way and all the obstacles and struggles you overcame to get to where you are now. Your audience might be exactly where you were just a few years ago, and a framework to help them get similar results to yours may be exactly what they want and need. There's something about sharing your personal story of transformation that's inspiring, and at the same time relatable. Positioning yourself as the guide to a transformation your audience wants—and that you've personally experienced—really allows your students to put themselves in your shoes.

Consider things you wanted just a few years ago that you have today, whether it was a challenge you overcame or a goal or dream you achieved. Then ask yourself: *How did I make that happen? What specifically did I do to get where I am now?* That "you" factor might just be waiting in your answers to these simple questions.

Take Katrina, for example. Katrina was a busy pediatrician who found herself unhappy and unhealthy. She had no desire to start her own business, and those who knew her best would say she didn't have a single entrepreneurial bone in her body. But after years on the job, she felt exhausted and stagnant. Her first step in getting her life back was reclaiming her health—she implemented healthy habits and lost 50 pounds.

After successfully keeping it off, Katrina wanted to help other women do the same. She knew their struggles of eating on the fly and experiencing stress-induced weight gain from juggling an impossible schedule. So she took the same process she went through herself and started coaching other female physicians, creating a business that gave her a freedom she never had as a doctor.

Exercise #4:
The Magic Wand Question

A great way to determine a topic your audience is interested in is by asking them directly about something they struggle with or a desired result they'd like to have. If you don't quite have an audience yet, ask five friends and family who would be a good fit or who can give you good feedback. You can do this with what I call the magic wand question:

If you could wave a magic wand and make your biggest challenge with [insert your business area] *disappear, what would it be?*

If your idea was time management coaching, the question could be, *If you could wave a magic wand and have your biggest challenge with time management disappear, what would it be?* Or, *If you could wave a magic wand and have your day perfectly planned, what would it look like?* Or even, *If you could wave a magic wand and have everything on your to-do list done, how would that immediately change your life?*

The beauty of asking these types of questions is that when your audience responds, you not only get great intel on your idea, but you get it in *their exact words*—which gives you insight into the language that speaks to them most. What's more, you've now opened a conversation with them. This is your chance to start building relationships that turn into sales down the line.

Whether you get one answer back or hundreds, make sure to respond to as many as you can. You can put this into action by posting your question on social media or by reaching out to your email list if you have one (and if you don't, hang tight, we'll get to this in Chapter 8) and asking them to reply. This one question can help you learn so much about where your audience is struggling the most, so pay close attention.

DO THE WORK: THE POST-IT PARTY STRATEGY

Now that we've talked through a few strategies to get your creative juices flowing, let's put them into action.

1. **Review your answers from the four exercises above.** If you haven't done all four exercises yet,

use the answers you have—and schedule time to do the rest!

- Go back to the list of topics you wrote down in Exercise #1 above. (I told you we'd be using them later!) Reading over them, ask yourself: *If you couldn't fail, and money wasn't an issue, what would you do?*

- Review your answers from Exercise #2: What areas are already working? What am I being paid to do? What do my friends and family ask me for advice on all the time?

- Look at your responses to Exercise #3: Where have you made improvements in your life? What struggles have you overcome? What goals have you achieved?

- Review the responses you got in Exercise #4, when you asked your audience the magic wand question.

2. **Choose one topic that lights you up.** Remember, this doesn't have to be the be-all, end-all topic you're going to devote your life to! You're still exploring, so have an open mind.

- Schedule 20 minutes to review all your ideas.

- Highlight every idea that lights you up.

- Go through the other sweet-spot categories and circle the ones that align with your skills, a need you see in the world, and where there is profit potential.

- Choose the *one* topic that hits all the categories the most.

3. **Brainstorm your unique approach.**

    - Take a stack of Post-it notes and your favorite Sharpie. You want to position yourself somewhere you have a blank canvas, so either in front of a wall or mirror so you can stick all your Post-it notes up and see them clearly.

    - Set a timer for 20 minutes and begin writing down and posting every idea, story, piece of content, insight, and action item that comes to mind for your business. This is not a time to judge or edit. All ideas make it onto a Post-it note!

        Let's say you're a pediatric occupational therapist (OT) and you have a passion for helping parents find solutions to help their children enjoy food from an early age. If you meet one-on-one with clients, write down everything you currently do with them. If you ask a set of questions when you first meet with them, write down those questions. If you have tried-and-true strategies you go back to again and again, write those down.

        Or maybe you're not an OT, but you figured out a way to curb your own kids' picky eating—you got results! So in this step, write down the recipes you make, the strategies and techniques you used with your own children, and the mindset shifts you had to make for yourself and that you work on with your kids. The Post-it notes might look something like this:

        - Simple meal ideas

        - How to introduce cups: sippy vs. straw vs. open

- What constitutes a snack vs. a meal
- Baby-led weaning
- Foods that picky eaters actually eat
- The 100 Introductions Rule
- Safe foods
- Parent's role during mealtimes
- Eating together
- Story: Jack eating sushi
- How to prepare foods for different ages
- Premade snacks and pouches
- Beverages: milk, water, and juice
- Introducing utensils
- Messy eating
- Serving sizes
- Common mistakes parents make

4. **Organize your framework.**

   - Start looking for themes across all the different Post-it notes and organize them into groups based on these themes.

   - Ask yourself: *How might I share these ideas?* (Maybe you have a specific way to organize your day or week that you could turn into a day planner); or, *How might I set up a system I can duplicate with each client?* (Maybe you are a website developer and there's a specific process you undertake with each website); or, *How might I teach this topic?* (Maybe you are a beauty expert and you teach your students tutorials).

- Break your framework, system, or process down into step-by-step, bite-sized chunks that will make sense at the most basic level. What are the phases or steps it takes to deliver your product or service?

- If you see that a step is missing, add it in!

5. **Put your framework in order.**

- Take each group of Post-it notes and organize them in the appropriate order. What needs to be done first? What part of your approach helps set the foundation? Then what comes next?

- When you have everything in the right order, name each part of the framework. *Step 1: The Mechanics of a Meal.* Or, *Phase 2: The Basics of Toddler Psychology.*

COURAGE VS. CONFIDENCE

Before we move on, I want to applaud you for the courage it's taken to come this far. Doing the exercises in this chapter can be incredibly confronting—they force us to face our deepest fears of being unworthy and undeserving and of not having anything original to offer and not bringing value. But I can tell you one thing for sure: Your willingness to face that kind of discomfort speaks volumes about who you are and how successful your business can be. And of all the characteristics that will serve you well on the journey ahead, none is more important than courage.

Notice that I said *courage*—not *confidence*. There's a big difference between the two, a difference that I think gets a little lost in the sauce of online business advice.

Courage is something you *choose*. Confidence is something you *earn*.

In this way, courage has to come before confidence. Confidence is neither necessary nor expected at this stage. Courage, on the other hand, is required. When I started, I constantly second-guessed myself, never fully believing I belonged where I was and always comparing myself to someone whose business was light-years ahead of mine. If I'd understood that I had no business being confident back then, it would have eliminated so much worry, confusion, and overwhelm for me!

Courage is already deep within you. You wouldn't be reading this book if you weren't one of the brave ones. You've already taken a leap of faith, just admitting you want more. You're betting on yourself, even though you don't have solid proof that it will all work out in the end. You are following your dream even when you don't know the outcome. *That's* courage.

As you start stringing together small successes—and learning from your failures—courage slowly morphs into confidence. Confidence is the outcome of taking that courageous leap; it's what courage *becomes*, once you have enough proof and experience. With each win—your website goes live, your social media begins to attract your perfect audience, and you make your first sale online—your confidence naturally grows. But the failures contribute too. Every time you crash and burn and get back up again, your confidence gets stronger.

Confidence *will* come, but not right away. This is why I don't want you to try to "find your confidence" when starting out on your entrepreneurial journey. Instead, we have to rely on courage to get started. In her book *The 5 Second Rule*, motivational speaker Mel Robbins says it best: "Confidence in yourself is built through acts of everyday courage." If you want to feel confident, in control, and in charge of your own destiny, you, my friend, just have to take the first brave step.

Chapter 5

You Ain't for Everyone, Boo
How to Identify Your Ideal Customer Avatar

Millie was an English as a second language (ESL) teacher working with immigrant and refugee students at the middle school level. Like many teachers, Millie was constantly on the lookout for resources and techniques that would help her students learn more efficiently and effectively. After spending hours searching online, scouring teachers' forums and communities, she came up empty-handed. So she decided to take matters into her own hands and create her own resource for ESL teachers—something she knew she needed and could benefit many of her colleagues.

She initially focused on helping ESL teachers at all levels, creating a full curriculum for new ESL students arriving at any point in the school year to learn about their new environment. But week after week, she watched as her email subscriber list (people who had given her their email address to get access to the curriculum she created) stayed in the single digits. She wasn't gaining the traction she had hoped for. In fact, almost half of her subscribers were family members. The English teacher was at a loss for words.

As an entrepreneur, it's crucial to understand who you're talking to, who you're creating for, and who you're selling to. While most new entrepreneurs want to cast a wide net and attract the largest possible audience, it's important to find your niche and identify one person who best reflects the desires and challenges your audience is experiencing.

After years of trying to be everything to everyone, I learned my lesson. As a recovering people pleaser, I've always wanted my work to make *everyone* happy, support *everyone*, and make sure *everyone* feels seen and heard. And if I'm being brutally honest, I want to be *liked* by everyone. (I hate admitting that! I'm working on it!) The challenge is, when you're creating a business from the "everyone must like it" frame of reference, you're going to have to water down your message to appeal to all points of view. In the process, you're likely to end up with something bland and "nice" but not compelling.

After one particularly stressful day at work, I opened my Instagram to blow off some steam and scroll. But I made the mistake of looking at some comments on a recent post of mine. I had shared ways to promote an offer online and a few people chimed in that my strategies were weak, that I didn't know what I was talking about, and one person even tagged other accounts to follow for better advice! I started feeling hot and my heart raced. I immediately started questioning myself—*Were they right? Would other people see the comments and* think *they were right?*

I knew I had to call in reinforcements, and more often than not, I call Jasmine.

Jasmine Star and I first met at a mastermind for entrepreneurs. I'd been hired as a guest speaker to talk about how I had grown my business. The day of the event, I discovered that Jasmine was going to teach about social media. I was invited to sit in on the session, but I debated it. *I know social media like the back of my hand*, I remember thinking. *What could she possibly have to teach me?* But no sooner had the first few sentences crossed her lips—and if you know Jasmine, you know they crossed *fast*—than I realized she was someone special.

Her delivery is a mix of brilliant insight and tough love, giving you exactly what you need while urging you to take action . . . yesterday. I loved her intensity. From that day, we were fast friends.

That day I texted her an SOS, complete with screenshots of the comments. *Should I reply? Should I delete the post? Should I change my marketing strategy? How can I fix this situation so everyone will like me again?*

Her pithy and perfect response? "You ain't for everyone, boo."

If I'd been a cartoon, you would've seen a light bulb go on above my head. I had taken a bit of a stand in that post, and the people who liked it were *my people*. The ones who didn't? They would unfollow me and go find the right teacher for *them*. Instead of wanting to be everything to everyone at all times, Jasmine had reminded me that I have a specific audience.

It was exactly what I needed to hear at that moment. And it's something that all entrepreneurs need to hear when they're first starting out. To be an entrepreneur means choosing an audience and serving them to the best of your ability. Not just "any old audience" will do—you have to find the one that gets you, resonates with you, and wants to bring you along on their journey. It's not about making everyone happy; it's about expressing yourself honestly so you start to attract the *right* customer for you.

Trust me when I say that this has been an ongoing journey for me. Negative comments can still get under my skin, but deep down I am rooted in Jasmine's perspective: *I'm willing to not be for everyone.* Because what I want even more than to be liked is to help the entrepreneurs who need *my* unique take on business growth.

As we already discussed, no ideas are new—what makes any given teacher stand out from the crowd is how we *interpret and apply* our wisdom. Take the process of growing your list. There are literally hundreds of marketing experts out there teaching list growth strategies, including me! As I'll be teaching you in Chapter 7, one of the mainstays of my strategy is creating original, free content every single week. But there are plenty of people in this industry who don't agree. They believe that creating content once a month or when you feel like it is okay and that posting on social media is enough. They have their own way of growing their email lists, and it's different from mine.

If I wanted to appeal to everyone, I might say something like, "I suggest creating content on a weekly basis. That said, you could do it just once a month if that suits you better." But do you feel what that does to the teaching? It waters it down, makes it less powerful, and doesn't reflect my true feelings.

I know that creating content once a week isn't an easy task, and in fact takes a lot of work. Claiming it as one of the pillars of my growth strategy is risky because not everyone is willing to do it. But I believe in this strategy to my very core. It's served me and my students well, even though I'm sure I've lost subscribers because it's such a big ask. But that's okay by me, because I now have an audience full of *entrepreneurs who are willing to take regular action to grow their lists.*

If you're thinking, *But, Amy, if I get* that *specific, I'll be leaving out so many potential customers!* I get it. And it's very important to make sure your narrowed audience doesn't exclude potential customers based on preconceived notions or discrimination. (More on this in a bit.) But if you create a clear definition of who you are, what you're about, and the specific customer you want to serve, many more customers will find you than if you maintained the *I'm for everyone* approach.

You'll begin to hear, "This was exactly what I needed!" or "How did you read my mind?" This is how you build what I call the "know, like, and trust" factor. Your audience knows you're there and what you're offering, they like what they're seeing and consuming, and they develop trust that you will reliably deliver. That's when you know you've nailed it.

And if you're still not convinced, let's go back to my student Millie, the ESL teacher who was struggling to get her resources out to the right audience. After a few weeks, Millie was discouraged but determined not to give up, so she joined a Facebook group for secondary ESL educators. Once she engaged with the group, she quickly realized that middle and high school ESL teachers faced very different challenges with their students and curriculum creation than elementary school ESL teachers. She switched her focus to the older age groups, letting group members know about the specific curriculum guide she had created. Almost immediately, Millie increased her email list 10,000 percent and achieved open rates of 80 percent (which is almost unheard of) because she was willing to get specific about her audience.

So now it's your turn. But in order to get clear on your perfect customer, you first need to understand what an Ideal Customer Avatar is all about.

FINDING YOUR IDEAL CUSTOMER AVATAR

Let's start by defining the term. Your Ideal Customer Avatar is your one *perfect* customer, the person who wants the exact content, products, and services you will create.

Remember the sweet spot test from the last chapter, where you identified a struggle, challenge, desire, or need you see in the world? Your Ideal Customer Avatar has that *exact* struggle, challenge, desire, or need, and will benefit tremendously from what your business has to offer.

Your Ideal Customer Avatar may be based on a real-life person you know, or they may be a composite of different people, real or imagined. Many times, your Ideal Customer Avatar is actually a version of yourself, back before you figured out the solution you're now offering to your customers. Maybe it's one of your best coaching clients. Maybe it's a family member or friend.

I want you to start by visualizing your Ideal Customer Avatar, and whoever it is, real or imagined, I want you to keep this one person in mind as you go through this set of questions. If you get stuck, just think, *What would this person do or say or feel?*

- As it relates to your "you" factor or business topic, what is your Ideal Customer Avatar struggling with *right now*? What's their biggest pain point? If your topic doesn't solve a pain point, maybe it meets a *desire*. If so, what's your Ideal Customer Avatar's biggest desire?

- What does your Ideal Customer Avatar need to understand, be aware of, or believe before they are ready to purchase something from you?

- If your Ideal Customer Avatar was hesitant to purchase from you, what would be holding them back *right now*?

- As it relates to your "you" factor or business topic, what does your Ideal Customer Avatar want *more* of? For example, more time? More freedom? More money? More confidence? More calm? More connection? More joy?

- What *specific* transformation and/or results does your Ideal Customer Avatar want to achieve after they've benefited from what your business offers (i.e., your product or service)?

If you can answer these questions with some certainty, you have a good understanding of your Ideal Customer Avatar. If, however, you're feeling a little uncertain and need to do some additional investigating, you're not alone. Maybe you *thought* you knew your audience, but after going through these questions, you're not so sure. That's okay! Most of us need to dive a little deeper to get some clarity.

Your Ideal Customer Avatar will develop and become clearer as you interact with them online more often over time, but in the meantime, I have created a more in-depth list to help identify some of the specific characteristics of your Ideal Customer Avatar, as well as common patterns and themes that address how they think and feel.

YOUR IDEAL CUSTOMER AVATAR DEEP DIVE

Understanding your Ideal Customer Avatar is crucial to your business success. If you do the work now, you'll have a crystal-clear snapshot of who you're serving and what you can do for them. Your goal with defining an Ideal Customer Avatar is to be specific and comprehensive.

There are so many voices in the online space competing for everyone's attention, and without a laser focus on your messaging, you're likely to get lost in the sea of noise. When you create language that resonates with your Ideal Customer Avatar, it's incredibly easy to gain their attention, even in a busy, online world. Think through these *in detail* as you read through them, including jotting down notes, if it helps. We'll put these together in a cohesive way at the end of the chapter.

Content Consumption

What kind of content are they consuming? Are they readers? If so, what are their favorite books or blogs to read? Do they enjoy podcasts? Are they TV or movie buffs? If so, what shows and movies do they watch? Do they listen to music, and if so, what genres?

Personal Time

What do they like to do in their free time? Do they have hobbies or interests? Are they involved in organized extracurricular activities? Are they a part of any boards, associations, or committees?

Career

What do they do to earn a living? Is this something they consider a part of their identity, a mission or calling, or is it something they do to pay the bills? Do they have a specific occupation inside a specific industry?

Online Behaviors

Where do they spend time online? Are they using search engines, reading and responding to email, or making online purchases? How do they engage with social media? Are they scrolling or commenting? Do they prefer Instagram, Facebook, Twitter, TikTok, Pinterest, or LinkedIn? What specific, or type of, Facebook group or online community might they be part of?

Mentors

Who inspires them? Who do they learn from? What person, people, or community do they love to follow online? Why are they attracted to these people?

Level of Happiness

Are they happy with where they are in life? If they are, what's bringing them joy? If they're not, what is keeping them from achieving it? What are their life circumstances and what are the emotions they feel on a consistent basis? What is their biggest pain point or frustration in life? What keeps them up at night?

Specific Demographics

For the purposes of truly identifying your Ideal Customer Avatar, it might also help to know if there are specific characteristics that define them. For example, are you a doula who works with pregnant and postpartum women? Do you specialize in helping baby boomers with their investments so that they can get on track to retire? Do you help non-English speakers learn English to navigate the professional world?

* * *

Understanding all of this will help you narrow down important details about your Ideal Customer Avatar and allow you to get into their heads so you know exactly what they want and need as you create content.

CREATING AN INCLUSIVE IDEAL CUSTOMER AVATAR

In today's world we're having many long-overdue conversations about inclusion and exclusion. There are ways in which choosing an Ideal Customer Avatar *can* reinforce stereotypes and leave out potential customers who don't fit your (possibly too narrow) view of your clientele. Perhaps, for example, you provide wedding planning for couples—but up until now you've been focusing your efforts only on straight relationships. Or maybe you teach online entrepreneurs how to master the technology side of their business, but you realize you've been unconsciously talking to one gender or ethnicity or age group.

When going through the exercises in this chapter, I want you to think about your Ideal Customer Avatar. Then I want you to zoom out and ask yourself, is there an opportunity to be more diverse and inclusive? For years, my Ideal Customer Avatar was various stages of myself throughout my transition from employee to entrepreneur. In other words, a white woman in her thirties with a college education and a certain level of financial independence. While it allowed me to get incredibly intentional about my messaging, it also tended to leave large demographics out—people who could gain tremendous value from what I had to offer.

This doesn't mean you shouldn't create an Ideal Customer Avatar or think about that *one* perfect person when you're creating content, building your product, and writing marketing materials. But it does mean that there is an opportunity for you to include people of various ethnicities, ages, gender identities, ability, sexual orientations, family dynamics, religions, and beliefs in your messaging, as long as they have the need or desire for what you're offering and teaching.

Your customers can look different and have different life experiences, but they're all connected by the opportunity your product or service offers them. Because at the end of the day, what matters most is that you get them at their core and you take the time to understand what makes them tick, how they think, and where they are struggling.

Once you've created your Ideal Customer Avatar description in the exercise at the end of this chapter, I invite you to take a step back and see where you can adjust and update their story to ensure your insights are precise, but still comprehensive.

As an example of this in action, we can look at Thinx, creator of the period-proof underwear, who changed their slogan from "For Women with Periods" to "For People with Periods," to include the transgender community, acknowledging that menstruation is not a trait of, nor a defining factor of, a specific gender—and that not all women menstruate, and not all people who menstruate identify as women. In my own business, I rewrote my Ideal Customer Avatar descriptions so that they weren't all women in corporate careers, around the same age and race with similar family situations, and it's helped me to be more inclusive in both my content creation and marketing.

WHAT TO DO IF YOU'RE STUMPED

If you've gotten to this point in the chapter and you're thinking, *Amy, I don't know the answer to* any *of these questions!* I want you to take a deep breath and know there's nowhere to go from here but up! Whether you're just starting out and don't have a social following, you've dreamed of getting a client or two on the side but haven't quite landed them yet, or you just don't have the experience of engaging with your Ideal Customer Avatar to see what's resonating with them, it's understandable that you would be having a hard time. So here are a few tips to learn about your audience when you don't have one yet.

1. **Be resourceful.** Your business idea didn't come from nowhere. You've got ideas in you, you just have to get focused. Take some educated guesses and refine as you learn more. Bounce ideas off friends and family. Research online. Just start somewhere.

2. **Search online communities and forums.** If you had to take a guess, what's a Facebook group your Ideal Customer Avatar might be a part of? Start there and read comments, look at posts, see what's getting the most engagement. Type a keyword search on Reddit and see what's trending or getting the most traction.

3. **Look at a similar audience.** Find someone who's already in your niche or the industry you're looking to get into, who has an audience, and see what they're saying. What type of content is resonating? What types of questions, frustrations, or even celebrations are showing up in the comments?

4. **Network with your Ideal Customer Avatar.** Go to events they are likely to attend. Talk to them. Find out more about who they are, what excites them, what they're working on, where they are struggling, what their dreams are, and where they might be stuck.

DO THE WORK: BRING YOUR IDEAL CUSTOMER AVATAR TO LIFE

Once you've visualized what your Ideal Customer Avatar wants and needs, and you've imagined a comprehensive list of characteristics about your Ideal Customer Avatar, I want you to start to write their story. And not just in your mind. I want you to write (or type) it out! Inside my business, I have a written profile of the Ideal Customer Avatar for each of my product lines. And my team and I remind ourselves who this person is every time we go to write an email or a training, or to create something new to inspire them. Here's a snapshot of our Ideal Customer Avatar for my signature program, Digital Course Academy:

Meet Dana—aspiring entrepreneur, 39-year-old single mom of two, burning the midnight oil while being an all-around badass go-getter

Dana is a smart, driven, ambitious woman. For a year now, she's been holding down her nursing job while taking care of her family and working to make a business out of what most people would call a hobby: her cozy knitted sweaters. Dana's always been the type to keep her head down and get the work done, no matter what the challenge is at hand.

But fast-forward another year and Dana's side hustle isn't quite giving her the freedom, flexibility, and financial abundance she once hoped for. She created her knitting business with the intention of spending more time with her kids and finally being able to leave her now part-time job once and for all, but she finds most days amounting to a frustrated plea of "There's only one of me!"

Dana's ready to shift her business model away from selling her hand-knitted sweaters—where her revenue is capped by the number of sweaters she can produce—toward a model that generates revenue even while she's nursing, taking care of her family, or enjoying herself.

She realizes that a digital course would be perfect for two reasons: First, it will help people learn to knit beautiful sweaters for themselves. Second, it will allow her to reach her revenue goals without feeling so stretched for time. Not only does she have a few course ideas and a solid understanding of her audience, she's got a proven track record, a wealth of knowledge in her niche (she's been knitting since her grandmother first taught her 27 years ago), and most importantly, the desire to take action and make a big change.

On the flip side, Dana doesn't necessarily feel confident in her ability to teach others and show up as a leader in her space. Can she really make a healthy living with something like a digital course? The idea of letting go of the stability of being a nurse freaks her out.

Despite her hesitations, Dana is hyperaware of the success other service providers turned course creators enjoy, and she knows a digital course is likely the solution to her business woes. If she had a proven step-by-step system to follow, taught by someone who knows exactly what she's going through, she'd finally feel confident in her ability to create and launch a course.

She may not know where to start or where she'll find the time to create a digital course, but there's one thing Dana knows for sure: she can't continue trading time for money and crossing her fingers that someday she'll have the freedom and flexibility that'll allow her to be fully present with her family. Once Dana has a clear road map that tells her exactly what needs to happen to make her digital course dreams a reality, nothing will stop her from creating a business and a life that reflects her values.

So now it's your turn. I want you to get out a fresh piece of paper or open up a new Google Doc and start writing.

- What is your avatar's name?

- What is their life like right now?

- What are they looking to change?

- What problem are they trying to solve?

- What transformation are they looking to achieve?

Spend some time and get creative—even though this exercise is only for your eyes, you'll be referencing this description again and again inside your business as a reminder of who you're serving. Use all the information you've brainstormed throughout this chapter. The more details you can capture, the more connection you will feel to this person as you are building the rest of your business.

DO THE WORK: VALIDATE YOUR IDEAL CUSTOMER AVATAR

When you have an avatar that feels right to you—*or* if you're still struggling to get through the first list of questions—I want you to get out and actually talk to this person. Even though you might have imagined them, your Ideal Customer Avatar exists in real life. Talk to that coaching client or colleague who would be perfect for your product or service. Reach out to your friends and family members and see if they know anyone who would be a good fit or get referrals from peers in your industry. Ask your social media followers if they would be willing to jump on a call with you. To figure out who to meet with, think about the people you *want* to work with. This is your *Ideal* Customer, after all.

When I created my membership experience, I drafted a story for my Ideal Customer Avatar, and then I actually sent it, word for word, to a student of mine, someone inside my community who I knew would be perfect for the product. I asked if it resonated with her, and she was able to point out some valuable distinctions that I wouldn't have known about if I'd just created a story on my own— distinctions that helped me tremendously when creating content for the membership and marketing it.

Aim to schedule at least two to three (the more, the better) 15- to 20-minute validation calls with people you think might be your Ideal Customer Avatar. The goal of these calls is twofold: (1) Uncover insights, fears, concerns, challenges, experiences, wants, and needs of your audience. (2) Determine whether you are on target with your "you" factor or business topic. Remember, one of the factors in the sweet spot test is the profit potential. Are people willing to pay for what you are offering? If something is off or is just not resonating, these conversations will give you more clarity and insight so that you can further develop your idea.

When you have your validation calls, listen more than you talk. See if the avatar description you created resonates with them. Ask open-ended questions to help you understand their wants, needs, and pain points. Questions like:

- Tell me about your [topic that relates to your business topic, e.g., "dating life," if you're a matchmaker] as it looks now.

- What are your biggest frustrations related to this topic? Where do you feel stuck? Why do you think this has been a struggle for you? How long has this been a struggle for you?

- What has stopped you from taking action in this area? What have you already tried that has not worked?

- Have you ever searched online for solutions? Did you take action from anything you found?

- If I could wave a magic wand and get you the results you are after, what would those results look like?

- How would you feel if you could get a solution to this challenge? What would life look like for you?

- Think about how you've learned best in the past. What are some of the common elements that have really made a difference for you?

- Where do you spend most of your time online (e.g., Facebook, Instagram, Twitter, TikTok, Google search, email)?

- Who are your favorite influencers in this area? What are your favorite accounts to follow? What do you like about them?

- Have you ever purchased a product or service related to this topic?

  - [If no] What's stopped you from investing in this further?

  - [If yes] Were you able to use it to get results? What was valuable about the product or service? What didn't work? What did you pay?

Keep in mind the specific words they use. These are a gold mine for your future copy, emails, sales pages, and social posts, so take lots of notes. You might even see if they would be okay with you recording the call. The actual language they use is what will resonate most, so as you begin to create your product or service and write your marketing messages down the road, you can come back to these specific words and phrases and integrate them throughout. These calls give you a glimpse into the mind of your Ideal Customer Avatar—don't take that lightly!

The goal here is to make sure that all the work you did in identifying your "you" factor and Ideal Customer Avatar can be validated by real people. If you discover that you are off in any part of your description, make sure to update it.

Now, if all of this avatar talk has your head swirling and you find you're worried about doing it "right" or perfectly, you're not alone. When I was first figuring out who my Ideal Customer Avatar should be, I worried I would lose time, money, and work if I didn't get it perfect the first time out. But over the years, that mindset has softened—a lot. Being hard on ourselves helps nobody.

With that in mind, I want to share a really helpful lesson I learned from my friend, life coach Brooke Castillo. I'd invited her onto my podcast to talk about the art of taking action. Only a few minutes into the interview, she stunned me and all my listeners by encouraging us to do B-minus work. Now, I literally got straight As in high school and college—my dad actually *paid* me for good grades—so you can only guess my reaction to this concept. *B-minus work?! NO WAY.* But Brooke had a solid argument.

Putting out B-minus work can help change your audience's lives. Whereas work that you don't produce at all—because you're frozen by the need to do it perfectly—does nothing in the world.

So I want you to set your fears aside. You don't have to do this perfectly. I don't want your desire to be perfect to keep you from choosing an Ideal Customer Avatar and *testing it out today.* This process is meant to help you get clear on your customer and their needs before you do the full rollout of your business.

Choosing the avatar is the fail-safe itself, making sure you don't launch a whole suite of services or products that won't resonate with your audience. It's okay if you miss the mark on your first, or even your tenth, try. It's better to learn that now than after you've done a ton of work. Revisiting and refining your Ideal Customer Avatar is just part of the process; be open to changing it as necessary.

Now get out there and start talking to people. From here on out, especially as you transition from where you are now to where you want to be, allow for some B-level work. (I know Brooke says B-minus, but I can't help myself—I still aim for B-plus, and you can too!) Because your audience *is* out there, and they are waiting for exactly what you have to offer.

Chapter 6

The Ugliest Website on the Internet
How to Build Your Website

A mira became a lawyer after watching her father pour his blood, sweat, and tears into his business, only to get hit with a $90,000 lawsuit and see his whole career come crashing down. Watching her family struggle inspired her to help other entrepreneurs avoid making the same mistakes her father had. But working as a nine-to-five lawyer, Amira realized she was limited in the number of people she could help.

Determined to make a bigger impact for business owners who needed to protect their life's work with the law, she started a side hustle and built a website to sell her done-for-you legal templates. By creating an online presence where her audience could purchase template bundles depending on what stage of business they were in, she was able to make the same amount of money in one *day* that she was making in a month at her full-time job.

This chapter is all about finding your very own home on the Interwebs: your business website. After teaching thousands of newbie business owners, I know you may be thinking, *Do I really even need a website? Can't I just rely on my social media channels instead?* The answer is an enthusiastic YES followed by a resounding NO.

If you want to build an online business, you absolutely need an online presence in the form of your *own* website. A Facebook page, Instagram business account, or YouTube channel is not enough, because they aren't *yours*. Relying on a platform owned and operated by a corporation other than your own puts you at huge risk. Their policies, algorithms, pricing, and guidelines can change dramatically from one day to the next. What you need is a steady, stable central hub that *you* control. That's a website, full stop.

Here in the digital age, your site is your business card, your brochure, and the place would-be customers can come for a sample of what it's like to work with you. And while it should be a simple process, you wouldn't believe the mistakes I've seen new entrepreneurs make as they build their first websites (myself included!). If you're at that precipice yourself, I'm happy to steer you away from some of these rookie fails. And if you already have a website, that's okay too: let's make sure it's the best it can be. Here we go!

THE UGLIEST WEBSITE ON THE INTERNET (MINE)

When I say I had the ugliest website on the Internet in my first few years in business, I'm not joking. A gray header. My name in black with a white shadow behind it. Graphics created using PowerPoint. Clashing typefaces. A mismatched color palette. Half of the blog post pages with a number in the title, half not. An "About Amy" section that lived in the footer, featuring a photo of me half smiling and looking down.

Looking back at some of my old blogs, I cringe at the images I used to illustrate each post. In one, I had a slab of meat hanging from a hook! *A slab of meat.* I'm blushing even as I write this.

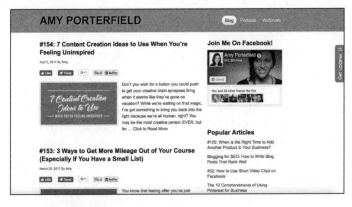

Obviously, my goal with this story is not to encourage you to build a mediocre website. In fact, I'd love for you to have a beautifully designed site that consistently converts—in other words, turns visitors and viewers into subscribers, customers, and students. But that kind of site can take months and months to build, not to mention truckloads of cash.

Instead I stand by a belief I've held since I first went out on my own: you don't need a fancy website with all the bells and whistles in order to be successful. Since I started my company, I've restructured and rebranded my website *three* times! A website is an ever-evolving thing, and whatever site you build today is not going to suit your business three or five years down the road. So why put the time, energy, and money into building a top-of-the-line site before your business is off the ground?

I've seen too many new business owners end up having to completely overhaul their high-cost "starter" site a year later because their business shifted in a new direction. Don't let that be you. Give yourself permission to keep it simple on your first site. The *function* of your website is a thousand times more important than the *form*. As ugly as my first site was, it *worked* for my customers.

When it comes down to it, you only need to answer two important questions to make your site functional.

Question 1: What is the goal of your website? Your website should have a very clear function in the ecosystem of your business. What are the messages you want to communicate to your visitors? In other words, how will they know they're in the right place once they arrive? How do you want your visitors to feel when they land on your website? Excited, inspired, seen, supported? What are the main functions you want your website to have?

Maybe it's your online "business card," a place for potential customers to find your contact information and reach out to you. Maybe the site is a storefront, where they can purchase courses, e-books, or physical products. If you offer a service like coaching or graphic design, your site might allow customers to get a taste of your work and decide whether you're the right fit for them.

Question 2: Where do you want to lead your customers? The purpose of your site is not only to share what your business is about—it's a place where you can add value to your visitors' lives and ultimately turn them into paying customers. So you need to think about their site visit as the first step in a clear process. Once they land on the website, then what? Where do you want them to focus first? What's the next step after that? How can you make it easy for people to navigate in the direction that will bring them the most value? This visitor journey is ultimately how you convert web *traffic* into web *business*, and it couldn't be more important.

To give you a clear understanding of what I mean by "visitor journey," let me give you an example from my own site. Let's say someone is listening to an episode of my *Online Marketing Made Easy* podcast. I always mention the URL for the show notes page, which is where they can read an overview of the episode's content and access any links and resources mentioned in the episode. Once they land on the page, they can immediately replay the episode and read a summary of what they'll learn.

As they scroll down through the page, they will be prompted to engage in a few ways, like getting access to a free resource related to the show topic (such as a checklist), reading a transcript of the episode, or rating, reviewing, and subscribing to the podcast. In addition, they will get recommendations of other episodes they might be interested in, which will lead them to the show notes pages for those episodes. They can even search through my entire catalog of episodes to find content they're interested in. Each of these steps encourages the audience to stay on my website and continue interacting with me and my content.

As you can see, the visitor experience is much more important than the site's visuals. At the same time you may be asking, "But can I still make it beautiful, Amy?" *Of course.* In fact, in the 14 years since I started my business, tons of new platforms have popped up to help you DIY simple, beautiful, *and* functional websites with minimal technological know-how.

Of course, go ahead, browse the fancy sites of more well-established businesses for inspiration. But when it comes to building your own, create the most basic site that fulfills your goals. You can 100 percent get the site you need by doing it yourself. And if you're shaking your head no right now, thinking you aren't tech-savvy enough to DIY, keep reading. I'm here to walk you through every seemingly intimidating step, so you can see it's totally doable after all.

GOING LIVE

Once you understand what you want your website to do for your customer, you have the map you need to start building it. First things first, you have to select a hosting service and a domain name. The hosting service essentially gets your website live on the Internet so that the rest of the world can access it. They "host" your website on their server, making it accessible and supporting the traffic that comes your way. They also provide storage space to house all of the assets that live on your website, including text, images, videos, and all other media.

> **For examples and my current favorite picks,
> visit www.twoweeksnoticebook.com/resources.**

Your domain name is the URL that people use to navigate to your site. This is typically your company's name, or if you are creating a personal brand, your first and last name. Which you choose depends on how central *you* want to be to your business and brand. Be aware that if you use your name—and down the line you want to step back from the business—you might need to consider rebranding.

On the other hand, if you're not 100 percent sure about the business you're starting, using a tentative business name may trigger the same need to rebrand later in the game. Which is why I also recommend steering away from product-specific URLs.

Let's say you teach parents how to take stunning pictures of their children without any photography background, and you sell presets (i.e., custom filters) to help them. I would caution you away from using www .familyphotopresets.com as your main URL since that is only one of the products you provide. And while I would definitely look into purchasing the URLs in the names of any key products you offer (like www.familyphotopresets .com or www.daylightportraitpresets.com) so someone else doesn't take them, I always recommend having these product addresses redirect to a main URL reflecting something more permanent, like your name or your established brand.

To see if the domain you'd like to use is available, you can search for it on a domain hosting site like GoDaddy .com. If it's not, and you're just starting out, I recommend looking for an alternative rather than paying through the nose to buy a URL that's already been claimed. Things change a lot in the first year or two of business, so I would hate for you to throw money away buying a claimed URL for a business name you may ultimately want to change.

If the .com address with your name or business name is taken, try a different extension (there are many to choose from these days, including .info, .pro, .live, .inc, and .store) or use a different version of the URL, like purchasing DrJaneSmith.com if JaneSmith.com is not available. That said, if you're a little more established, already have a brand or online presence, and have the money to spare—you can always make a bid on a claimed URL and see what happens!

Now that you know where your site will live and what its address will be, you need to determine which platform you want to use to build it. You have three options: the "all-in-one" site builder, the hybrid site builder, and the fully DIY method.

An "All-in-One" Site Builder
(Difficulty Level: Easy)

An all-in-one website platform delivers exactly what the name implies—where everything you need to set up your site is available and easy to implement. You pay a fee, and the builder walks you through a set of basic choices to help you create a turnkey website.

As a new entrepreneur, a builder like this is the perfect solution. They are user friendly, meaning just about anyone can use them without needing to hire a designer or web developer. They offer page builders, templates, seamless integration with popular software, and support. The downside is that these platforms tend to be more expensive than the other options listed here. As you start to grow, they can also lack some of the advanced options a more customized platform will give you—meaning that if you want options that aren't available "off the shelf," you may have to hire a web developer to rebuild your website on a more flexible platform.

For a breakdown of "all-in-one" site builders, make sure to check out my online resource hub at www.twoweeksnoticebook.com/resources.

The "Hybrid" Site Builder: WordPress (Difficulty Level: Easy to Moderate)

Almost a third of all websites online—including my own, and more than half of the top 100 fastest-growing companies in the U.S.—use a website creation platform called WordPress. WordPress is an open-source system that allows anyone to create and manage a website and its content without knowing anything about web development or programming. Building your website with WordPress is the middle-of-the-road, hybrid solution.

WordPress offers templates similar to the all-in-one platforms mentioned above, but it's much more flexible—so down the line, you can hire a web developer to upgrade your site and add more functionality if you need it. At the same time, the back end is easy to navigate, so it's completely doable for you to update your site content yourself, without having to call in a developer to do it for you. WordPress offers many design elements (like colors, fonts, and layouts) to choose from, as well as more advanced options and plugins (software that adds functionality to a site, for example a video player) for more complex features, making it a versatile option.

The Do-It-Yourself Method (HTML)
(Difficulty Level: High)

Alternatively, you can go the DIY route, building a website from scratch using HTML code. HTML, or HyperText Markup Language, is a programming language used to structure a web page and its content so that it can be displayed in a web browser to the general public. With this method, you're after control and flexibility. You don't want to be married to any particular service provider, and you want to customize your website however you'd like. This solution is perfect for anyone who has experience in coding or web development and wants to save money by doing it themselves.

But if you need to hire a web developer to build and maintain the site for you, it can actually end up being more expensive and time-consuming than the previous two options. For a brand-new entrepreneur who doesn't have coding expertise, I typically recommend one of the first two options.

* * *

None of these options is any better than the other; whichever you choose will ultimately get you to the same place—a functioning site that generates revenue. When you're first starting out, you might want to make things as easy as possible for yourself and opt for an all-in-one builder. Alternatively, if you enjoy rolling up your sleeves and figuring out the back-end technology and you have time to do so, one of the other options might work best for you. In the end, the choice is yours!

THE FOUR ESSENTIAL WEB PAGES

Once you've selected a web host, bought your domain name, and chosen your building approach, it's time to start building! There is no need to overwhelm yourself with complicated site maps and 20-page websites. As I said earlier, a website is an evolving thing. You can always adjust and update your website as time goes by and your business grows. But here, as you're just getting set up, there are only four essential pages I recommend having on your website: your home page, your about page, your contact page, and your blog page.

Home Page

Your home page is the first page of your site where your potential customers will most often land when they search for you and your business. You can think of it as the front door to your online world, so you want it to be inviting. Its primary function is to capture the visitor's attention and encourage them to dive deeper with you and the content of the site.

I suggest using this online real estate for three main things:

1. Your "you" factor: tell your visitors right up front about the problem you're solving, who you're serving, and how you're helping them achieve the results they desire.

2. A compelling image: something that best represents what you do and connects with your visitors. If you're the face of the company, I recommend including an image of you.

3. An opt-in: a place for visitors to exchange their email addresses for valuable content with a clear call-to-action button. We'll go into more detail about this in Chapter 9.

While the goal of your home page is to make an impression on your visitors, it's no longer the sole point of entry to your site. Online behavior today shows that many visitors will arrive on your site via links from social media, search engines, or other sites. Since a user may land directly on your blog, your about page, or any other page of your site, every page on your site needs to get just as much attention as the home page.

About Page

Unlike my first website, where "About Amy" was in the *footer* of the home page (read: nobody ever saw it), I recommend you create an entire page where your potential customers can go to learn more about who you are, why you do what you do, and whether you're the right person to guide them toward the transformation they're looking for.

Contrary to being an "afterthought," your about page is one of the most important pages on your site for *selling*. Your about page offers a huge opportunity for you to build a connection with your Ideal Customer Avatar. This is where you get to introduce yourself, tell your story, establish credibility, and build that "know, like, and trust" factor.

Don't shy away from personal stories that give your audience a glimpse into why you do what you do or how you started on your pathway to entrepreneurship. Instead, share candid photos showing your personality or, my personal favorite, a snapshot of a beloved pet. Use this page to show off your personality or that of your company, and be genuine, not generic.

Contact Page

This one is pretty straightforward: make it easy for your customers to contact you by including a page dedicated to getting in touch. You can simply list your email address, social media links, or phone number. Or, if the site-builder platform you chose offers a "contact form" option (most do), you can make it easy for visitors to write you a note right there on the page itself, which will be sent directly to your email.

Blog Page

The term *blog* is a bit of a misnomer in the way that you can use this page. More than just being a blog, it's a place for you to *house your content*. We'll go into this more in the next chapter, but as you create content for and build a relationship with your Ideal Customer Avatar, you'll need somewhere to consistently direct traffic to access that content.

And whether you write a blog, record a podcast and create episode show notes, or host weekly office hours and post a summary of each session, you'll need one main blog page to house this content. The main page will be a directory of links—often with a search functionality provided by your web builder—so readers can find exactly the topic they're interested in and then click through to read, listen, or watch.

This content is especially important because the more content is housed on your website, the higher your search engine optimization will be. In the simplest terms, SEO is a marketing strategy to increase your web search ranking.

When someone types specific keywords into a search engine that relate to your business, product, or service, you want your content to pop up on their results page.

The majority of all web traffic comes from search engines, so the higher your site ranks in the results for relevant keywords, the more likely someone will find their way to your site and ultimately engage with you in some capacity. When done right, having a lot of great free content on your site will increase both the quality and quantity of traffic to your website.

THE FIVE WEBSITE ELEMENTS TO FOCUS ON

One of the most important functions of your website is to communicate your brand—what your business is all about and what sets it apart from other businesses. Your brand should be consistently communicated through five key elements: design, copy, photography, navigation, and what I call the "next steps" of your site. Let's take a minute to explore how each element is used.

Stellar Design

While my first website still converted visitors to customers, think about how much *more* effective it might have been if it hadn't been eye-bleedingly ugly. In other words, a modern, professional, and aesthetically pleasing design *helps*. It's the first thing visitors see when they land on your website, even before they see your content, products, or services.

If you've spent some time thinking about your branding, make sure your website matches how you want your business to look and feel, in terms of fonts, colors, layout, and imagery. If you haven't worked on your branding yet, don't worry—there are great website templates and design structures that you can use as a base for your own site. Just remember, less is more, so keep it clean, not cluttered.

Compelling Copy

Copy in this context refers to any text on your website *outside of* the content on your individual blog pages—so for example, all the text on your home page and about page are part of your site's "copy." Nothing could be more important to your efforts to engage and add value to your visitors. As entrepreneur and designer Jeffrey Zeldman says, "Content precedes design. Design in the absence of content is not design, it's decoration."

You want copy that's concise, persuasive, easy to read, and clearly reflective of your message. Syntax, grammar, and spelling are key to presenting your work in its best possible light, so make sure every single piece of copy on your site has been edited and proofed. If this isn't your strong suit, invest in a professional editor, or get a friend or family member to help you out. Also, if you're not a writer, think about outsourcing your copywriting to a professional marketing copywriter who produces snappy and driven messaging for a living.

Standout Photography

Images are essential to any website. When done right, they draw your visitors in and connect them even more deeply with your content. One of my mentors, the author and productivity expert Michael Hyatt, says that content designed to include compelling images can average 94 percent more total views than words alone. Yes, you read that right: 94 percent!

Take the time to produce or find the right images to enhance your content. If you're not set up for producing your own great shots, there are some amazing stock sites that you can use to find high-quality images. Just make sure to use the images according to their licensing.

For a full list of great photography resources, visit www.twoweeksnoticebook.com/resources.

Simple Navigation

Have you ever found yourself completely lost, trying to navigate a site that has a dozen menus, tabs, and links? I'm pretty sure this maze is not part of the look and feel you want for your business! On the contrary, I'm guessing you want your visitors to find what they're looking for without much effort. If so, the key is *simple navigation*.

Navigation is the path or flow through which visitors move on your site, and it includes how your visitor gets from one page to the next. When done right, navigation can increase the time a visitor or customer stays on your site. The best site navigation is typically structured through a well-organized, intuitive, and easy-to-use menu that lists all available pages. Keep your navigation short and sweet, focused on the four essential pages we just learned about: home page, about, contact, and blog.

Next Steps

Sometimes referred to as the "call to action" or CTA, the "next step" is the action you want your visitor to take after arriving at your website. Examples might include "contact me," "schedule a call," "learn more," or "register." When you're just getting started, I recommend your next step to be signing them up for your email list. (Not sure what an email list is? Hang tight—I'll go into it in more detail in Chapter 8.) An engaged email list is the single most important asset you can have in your business, and your website is a great tool to help build it, especially when you're first starting out.

Whatever next step you choose, you need to make it very clear—and design your site so it's hard for your visitors *not* to do it. Generally speaking, next steps show up as "buttons" that visitors can click throughout the website. Make sure opportunities to take those steps are present and accessible no matter where the visitor is on your site, ensuring your visitors can do it as quickly and easily as possible.

DO THE WORK: DRAFT YOUR ABOUT PAGE

From choosing a hosting company to registering your domain name to choosing a building strategy, we've already discussed several actions you can take to get your first website underway. But to help create some momentum right now, I'm giving you five prompts to get started on your about page. I suggest you find a quiet spot, give yourself 45 minutes of uninterrupted time, and use these prompts to draft your own story.

1. How did you get involved doing what you're doing?

2. Why should someone work with you? What benefits do you/your business/your product or service provide your audience?

3. How do you want to be seen in your industry and/ or by your customers? What kind of impact do you want to make?

4. What's a challenge you overcame that could help your audience?

5. What was an aha moment you had along your journey that's helped you get to where you are now?

Now take yourself on an online field trip, visiting the about pages of three to five influencers or organizations in the same space your business is in. Notice how they structure their pages. How do they use their personal stories? What else do they include?

Next, take your first draft from the prompts and begin to revise it into an actual about page you could be proud of. When writing this page and all the content for your website, remember to keep your Ideal Customer Avatar in mind. (If you need a little inspiration, check out my about page at amyporterfield.com/about.)

If you're starting to shake in your boots a bit at the thought of putting yourself out there in the form of a website, you are not alone. It's freaking *scary* to be that visible. But it will be worth it. *The goal is to do something.* Get into motion, and with that motion will come clarity. Every entrepreneur I know cringes when they think back to their early efforts, but we all have to start somewhere. Which is what the next chapter is all about—so let's dive into content creation in three . . . two . . . one!

Chapter 7

Content Is Queen
How to Create Badass Content Consistently

For the better part of five years after I went out on my own, I had very little strategy around regularly providing value to my audience. At first I worked one-on-one with clients, who paid hourly for my services. Once I stopped consulting, I went straight into creating my first paid product: a digital course. I dabbled in writing blog posts, sometimes publishing twice a month, sometimes once a month. But I struggled to write each one, procrastinating and sometimes giving up altogether. I never really felt like I knew *what* to write about, and I wasn't making *money* from it, so why spend time doing it?

Occasionally I would send a standalone newsletter to my email list. More often than not, the newsletter would tell a story or offer some piece of advice rather than linking to a blog or other content on my website. And even once I started my *Online Marketing Made Easy* podcast, I only released one or two episodes a month on no set schedule, sometimes even skipping a month. But when I started producing my podcast on a regular weekly schedule two years later, my profits nearly tripled.

Instead of asking your audience to trust you—and blindly part with their hard-earned money just because you tell them it will be worth it—why not make the process a whole lot easier on them by delivering value *first*? No matter what product or service you offer, nothing helps build raving fans more than delivering quality free content on a consistent basis.

I want to instill this mantra in your head: content is queen. Routinely releasing original content will allow your audience to get to know who you are, what you are about, and how they can work with you. And when your audience knows you, likes you, and, most importantly, *trusts* you, they'll be excited to exchange money to continue receiving the value and transformations you offer.

When you lead with impact and create results for your customers, the money will follow.

CHOOSE YOUR WEEKLY CONTENT PLATFORM

Your content platform is the means through which you'll share valuable content with your audience.

To avoid overwhelm, I recommend choosing a single platform. Down the road you can start repurposing content across multiple platforms, but keep it simple as you're starting out. The best piece of advice I can give you at this stage is to choose a content platform that sounds *fun* to you.

Consistency is the only rule, but choosing a platform that feels like a slog will make it really hard to show up week after week. That said, there are *so* many ways you can deliver content consistently that there's bound to be one that lights your fire. So let me walk you through a few examples you might be able to get behind.

Writing a Blog

Are you a naturally talented writer who communicates better through writing than through verbal conversations? If the answer is yes, a blog might be the perfect fit for you. Blogs are a great entry point into the world of content creation. They're easy to produce (especially once you have your website set up), allow you to repurpose material you've already created, and require no filming or recording skills to create.

My student Audrey worked in the nonprofit world for 13 years. And she rocked it. When her colleagues were sporting old college sweatshirts and worn-out flip-flops, Audrey was the one who showed up each morning in the latest style, looking effortlessly pulled together.

Audrey knew she wanted to express herself in creative ways beyond just getting dressed every day. So she started a style blog, and it was love at first post. Audrey thrived in this digital space, playing around with current fashion trends and helping women feel more confident about themselves through her simple style advice. Even as a side hustle, Audrey's following started to explode. And within a few years, Audrey said good-bye to an organization she loved, embraced the fear of going out on her own, and entered the world of blogging full-time.

Recording a Podcast

It's safe to say that podcast listening is on the rise with no signs of slowing down. According to Edison Research, more than half of all Americans have listened to at least one podcast, with more than 176 million listeners tuning in weekly and an almost 30 percent growth in listeners between 2018 to 2021 alone.[1]

Because podcasts are audio only, they are easy to consume while engaging in other activities. They also help develop a connection between host and listener, because your audience hears your voice and can get a feel for your personality. Podcasting is my platform of choice—I've been recording episodes for my *Online Marketing Made Easy* podcast for almost 10 years, and my favorite part is that it feels like I'm having an intimate conversation with every listener.

Podcasting can take a little more time and savvy to set up initially. You'll need a mic, recording device, editing software, and if you plan to have guests, a way to record interviews. But once you're established, uploading to the major podcast apps is simple.

Producing Video

Video hit the Internet like a tidal wave more than a decade ago and is here to stay. Videos account for 82 percent of online traffic,[2] where the video sharing site YouTube has more than 120 million unique visitors every single day,[3] and video-driven social media app TikTok surpassed Google as the most popular website in 2021.[4] It's no surprise, since video creates both a visual and auditory connection with your viewer, allowing you to share your personality and expertise in multiple ways and form a deeper relationship with your audience.

Some options for delivering video content include hosting a weekly vlog or video show or using a social media platform like TikTok, Instagram Live, LinkedIn Live, or YouTube. A great example of a video show is MarieTV, hosted by my friend and early mentor, Marie Forleo. It's an award-winning show with hundreds of episodes on how to build an online business—so it's both an example of a great video show and a great source of information for you!

Building an Online Community

An online community is a group of people with a shared interest or purpose who communicate with each other via the Internet. As a content platform, an online community is a great place to post videos, create interactive posts, answer questions, and host conversations between your members.

An online community can be as simple as starting a free, private Facebook group where people interested in your expertise gather to share information and hear from you. Or you can use specialized software platforms to create a customized site just for your members. You can check out www.twoweeksnoticebook.com/resources for my current recommendations.

My student Nicole created the Beauty Content Club, a free Facebook group for beauty professionals, entrepreneurs, and influencers to help them create engaging web and social media content to grow their business. She is able to deliver her own content and resources, like her Beauty Content Calendar and editable graphics, as well as foster a community and space to build connections for fellow content creators in the beauty industry.

Starting your own online community involves a few more steps up front, but once it's in place, you will have a highly targeted online space to cultivate real connections with your audience. Communities can take on a life of their own because content can be created by the people inside the community, increasing engagement, and the cultivation of real relationships between members. The downside, if you want to call it that, is that moderating a membership can take time and energy. But if you have the ability and are looking for a place to deliver content in a more interactive, group setting, an online community is a great platform to explore.

Hosting Q&As or Office Hours

Hosting Q&A sessions or "office hours" is an excellent way for your Ideal Customer Avatar to get their questions answered by you personally and in a timely fashion. You can deliver office hours live via video or on replay inside your private community or on social media, or post an audio or video recording of yourself answering questions your audience submitted in advance. The personal attention given to your audience makes this type of content a tremendous value add, and these sessions can make a big difference in helping your students get unstuck and continuing to move forward.

One of my students, Lindsey, is a dog trainer. She hosts a weekly "Ask the Trainer" Q&A inside her Paw Prints University, where she answers her audience's most pressing questions and helps them overcome the challenges they're having with their dogs. Not only is this a great way to provide value to her group members, but it helps Lindsey see what pain points her audience is experiencing, which is invaluable intel as she creates more content to help them in the future.

If *all* these platform options sound good to you, I caution you against going overboard. Instead, I highly encourage you to choose *one* platform and stick with it—for six months at least.

Don't do a blog post one week, then host office hours the next, and then throw in a random podcast episode the following week. Stick with what you do best and what best serves your audience. Commit to showing up on one platform come rain or shine, especially when you're just starting out, to help build a solid relationship with your audience where they will come to know what to expect from you. It will also help you stay focused and feel less overwhelmed, so you won't spread yourself so thin that you're liable to give up altogether.

When choosing your first platform, it's critical to keep your audience in mind. Pull out the work you did around your Ideal Customer Avatar from Chapter 5. Where do they like to hang out? How do they consume content?

For example, if your customers are busy, on-the-go working parents, a podcast might be best. That way they can listen while commuting or doing the laundry. If they're beginning-level knitters who need to see the exact way you're holding the needle or wrapping the stitch, then a weekly video tutorial might be the ticket. That way you can visibly show the technique, while you explain it. If they're avid foodies who want step-by-step instructions, you might want to deliver a written recipe blog with photos and ingredient lists.

FREQUENTLY ASKED QUESTIONS

Now that we're clear on different *ways* you can share your expertise and generate your audience's trust, let's go over some of the most frequently asked questions I get about content creation.

FAQ #1: How often should I share content?

I highly recommend that you consistently create new content once a week. This will allow you and your audience to get to know each other at a depth that's not possible if you publish content sporadically, with long breaks between each communication. When your potential customers are listening to you, watching you, or reading your words on a weekly basis, they will start to trust you and eventually build a relationship with you.

Take my student Meredith, for example. Meredith was always interested in health, fitness, and wellness, but straight out of college she found herself working as a corporate recruiter. She was burning out fast and the idea of creating her own business where she could do things her own way and coach people to their best health was very attractive. She wasn't exactly sure where to begin, but one day she decided to start sharing content via Facebook Live videos. Soon she was going live every week, helping viewers by answering their health questions "on the air." She was truly improving the quality of their lives, and it showed—her one-on-one coaching business took off.

FAQ #2: What content should I be sharing?

The quickest answer to this question is: share the content that answers your Ideal Customer Avatar's primary pain points and desires. In marketing terms, a "pain point" is a challenge, struggle, or fervent desire your customer has but doesn't know how to resolve on their own. You want to be their go-to solution for this issue, which starts with letting them know in no uncertain terms that you *get* them. You want them to see that you know what they're going through and you're here to help.

Now I know you may be thinking, *How the heck am I going to come up with new content to share every single week?* I feel you! When I first started, this was one of the biggest challenges I had.

To find out, go back to your Ideal Customer Avatar. Think about whoever you chose—whether it was a client, a family member, or you yourself at an earlier stage of your journey. What does this avatar want? What do they struggle with? What blocks are standing in their way? What can you teach them that will inspire and empower them? What myths do you need to dispel? What kind of content will pique their interest and strengthen their desire to learn more from you?

Now address what your customer is thinking, worrying about, and/or wishing for. And then give them what they *need* most.

As you interact with your Ideal Customer Avatar more, you'll get clear on the pain points and desires they have. Every time they comment on social media, ask a question during a live video or office hours, or write into your website's contact page, they will be giving you clues about their challenges. Over time you'll begin to see the same questions show up over and over, from person to person, and you'll start creating content specifically to address these questions.

The more you interact, the more your audience will quite literally teach you what content they want from you! But don't wait to understand every single detail about your audience to start creating content. What's most important is that you start somewhere and pay attention to the feedback you get. Keep a running list of the questions your Ideal Customer Avatar throws your way, and you'll never run out of ideas for content to share.

For example, I always listen to Glennon Doyle's podcast *We Can Do Hard Things* because every week she shares topics that are hugely relevant and important to me. I leave each podcast episode wondering, *How did she know exactly what I needed to hear today?* This feeling—that she's speaking directly to my pain point and giving me hope and solutions—keeps me coming back for more.

FAQ #3: What should I give away for free and what should I charge for?

When it comes to producing free content, my number one piece of advice is: *stack the value.* What I mean by this is to make sure you are offering your very best content for free. This is not the time to hold back; your weekly content should knock the socks off your audience. It should be something they *would* pay you for but are getting for free.

Great content might be thoughtful, helpful, enlightening, entertaining, relatable, compelling, experience-based, inspiring, and/or action oriented. Obviously it doesn't have to be all of these things at once! But aim to attain one or more of these qualities and you'll be on the right track.

You may think this sounds counterintuitive; shouldn't you save your best content for your paid product or service? Here's the thing—I built my business by giving away my best stuff for free. Ideally someone watches your weekly live video or reads your blog post and thinks, *Wow! This is so incredibly helpful. If she gives away this much value for free, imagine how powerful her paid stuff must be!* In that moment, you've given that person a visceral understanding of how much you can help them—both gaining their trust and very likely securing yourself a loyal fan and future customer.

To help determine the difference between your free content and paid product or service, let me share my rule of thumb:

> *Free Content:* Introduces the transformation your paid content offers and gives a taste of that transformation

> *Paid Product or Service:* Delivers the full transformation

Whatever your teaching, guidance, or expertise is, the value you're delivering is ultimately some sort of transformation. Whether you teach millennials how to manage their money, coach physicians on a system to get their paperwork done *during* office hours, or help creatives set up the operational side of their business, your audience will be fundamentally changed for the better by working with you or your products.

Your free content is what prepares your reader to be ready for the paid transformation. In most cases, this includes thoroughly explaining what they can expect to understand, gain, or be capable of doing after purchasing your product or service. What do they need to understand or believe in order to keep moving forward toward becoming your customer? What small wins can you guide them toward now, so they get a taste of the transformation they can expect with your paid content?

Then the paid content—your product or service—needs to deliver on the promises made in the free content. Your paid content will include your blueprint, formulas, road maps, and the full *how* for achieving the transformative experience your customer needs and wants.

Remember the Post-it Party strategy you worked on back in Chapter 4? In your paid product or service, you will include the process you laid out in detail for how your customer will actually do the work to get the results you're promising, from start to finish. Your free weekly content will add value, tease the *how*, and get your audience on the road to results, but it should not give away everything your paid offer includes.

For example, inside of my Digital Course Academy program, I have an 11-step Course Creation & Launch Framework. This framework is the entire process I teach my students to help them create and sell a digital course from scratch.

The first step in the framework is to make nine key decisions, and one of those decisions is around your course topic. In one of my past Digital Course Academy promotions, I released a podcast episode where six students shared their course topics and how they came up with their ideas. I also hosted a Facebook Live video where I taught different strategies for choosing a profitable topic for a course.

In both of these pieces of free content, I showed my students that they'd need a topic in order to create a course, and even shared a few strategies to start brainstorming topic ideas. This free content only addressed *one* of the nine decisions in the *first* step of an 11-step process, but it encouraged many of them to become paying customers by giving them a taste of the enormous value the full course offers.

BATCH YOUR CONTENT

Okay, you might be thinking, *I'm on board with what and how often to share. But how the heck do I make time to create all this dang content?* Good news: As much as I love to dream big and paint the best picture of possibility and opportunity, I'm also a realist who likes to work out plans and set things in motion quickly. I do this by *scheduling time to do the work.*

Remember the adage from Chapter 2, "It's not real until it's scheduled?" I live and die by this motto. You didn't come this far to just dream and hope it all comes together. You came this far to make things *happen.* Which starts with committing to creating regular weekly content to serve your Ideal Customer Avatar.

If that sounds daunting, it doesn't have to—thanks to a strategy I use called *batching.* Batching is the process of dedicating blocks of time to work on similar tasks, in order to decrease distraction and increase productivity. The goal is not to multitask but instead to intentionally choose similar tasks (like content creation) and focus on them for a specific period of time. For example, if you decided your weekly content will be a blog, you might sit down in one session, and over the course of a few hours, write four blog posts, one for each week, getting a whole month's worth of work done in one session. Batching eliminates content creation stress and overwhelm and allows you to produce more in less time.

Think of batching as a form of time management. In an article in the *Harvard Business Review*, leadership expert Peter Bregman notes that our productivity goes down by 40 percent when we attempt to focus on several things at once.[5] Oftentimes people brag about their ability to "multitask," but studies have shown over and over that rapidly switching from one task to the next actually kills our productivity.[6] Every time we become distracted, it takes an average of 23 minutes to regain that initial focus.[7]

I like to batch in three phases: first the batch planning session, second the creation of a content calendar, and third the actual content creation sessions.

Batch Planning Session

If batching is all about dedicating a set amount of time to do similar tasks, a "batch planning session" is a set amount of time dedicated to *planning* out those tasks. For me, this means a 30- to 60-minute block of time where I brainstorm eight weeks of free weekly content all in one sitting. I try not to overthink it; I just pick up a notebook and pen and start writing. If I ever get stuck, I go back to the notes I took from my validation calls with my Ideal Customer Avatar (page 93) and read over the questions, struggles, and challenges I've heard directly from them.

But if you don't have a list like this yet, don't worry. Just imagine the questions and struggles your Ideal Customer Avatar is likely having right now, and write down the solutions you can teach, exercises that would be helpful, and experts you might interview to give this customer a taste of the relief they're looking for.

Here are some tips to get you started on the planning session:

- **Start with a brain dump.** Write down any and all ideas that pop into your head. What topics would be beneficial to your audience? What content would enhance their lives? What are some of the questions your audience is already asking you? What are some of the questions your audience *should* be asking you but don't know to ask yet?

- **Check your calendar.** It's nice to tie your free content into upcoming holidays or special events, so look at the next two months for opportunities. For example, if you teach people how to organize their houses and you're creating free content for March, you could create a "Spring Clean-Out Checklist." If you're working on content for August or September, you could offer a "Back-to-School" guide to decluttering your kid's room.

- **Do some research.** Use Google or YouTube to type in key phrases that relate to your business and see what comes up on the first page of results. Since these results are directly tied to the answers people in your audience are searching for, this intel is gold, especially when you're starting out and haven't had a ton of interaction with your audience yet. Turn these results into topics you can write about.

  For example, let's say you teach watercolor painting to novice students. You might search for the phrase *beginner watercolor lessons*. If words like *easy*, *basic*, *techniques*, and *beginner* show up over and over on the first page of results—meaning the audience you're aiming for is looking for easy and basic techniques—you might consider creating a blog called "Three Easy Beginner Watercolor Techniques" or a video where you teach "Brush Basics for Beginning Watercolor Painters." Bonus tip: Scroll down the page to the section that says "Related searches" to see other popular topics that people are searching for within your niche.

Master the Content Calendar

Once you've created your list of content topics, having a clear plan of when everything will be released will eliminate the weekly scramble to get something published, allow you to be proactive and plan ahead, and give you the opportunity to align relevant content with specific events, holidays, or seasons. Creating this "content calendar" or "editorial calendar" is simple.

1. **Open a new document.** I like to use Google Sheets, but you can use Microsoft Excel or even just a piece of paper if you're old school like that.

2. **Create a table with four columns and eight rows** (a row for each week of content in this batch). At the top of each column write the following: Date, Topic, Notes, Platform.

3. **Fill in the chart.** In the "Date" column, write the date you want the piece of content to release. In the "Topic" column, record the topic you brainstormed during your batch planning session. Use the "Notes" section to record anything you might want to remember about the release of

this content—for example, if it's tied to a holiday or part of a monthly theme. Finally, use the "Platform" column to note where you'll be posting this specific content. If you're just starting out, this will be the platform you chose earlier in this chapter. As you grow, you might expand to more than one platform—posting a video to both Instagram and YouTube, for example.

Your completed content calendar should look something like this:

Date	Topic	Notes	Platform
Aug 21	Closet refresh: changing summer to fall wardrobes	Summer ending, moving into fall	Blog post on website
Aug 28	Tips to declutter your kids' rooms before they're back to school	School starts late August	Blog post on website
Sep 4	How to help keep your kids' school supplies organized	School starts late August	Blog post on website
Sep 11	What to do with all the water toys now that the beach days are over	Summer ending, moving into fall	Blog post on website

This content calendar has both proactive and reactive uses. Proactively, you can now create all this incredible content you've planned. Reactively, you'll now have a record of all the different content you've created, when it was released, and on which platforms. If you're ever looking for a specific piece of content in the future, you've already created a simple and searchable database.

I can't tell you how much time I used to spend searching my files to find a specific story or script. But now that I've created a content calendar for my podcast, everything is in one organized place that I can search whenever I need to.

Create the Content

Voila, your batch planning session has produced two months' worth of content ideas and you now have a neatly laid-out content calendar! Good job. The next step is to write/record/produce the content itself!

My suggestion is to batch—i.e., create or produce—four pieces of content at a time in one six-hour block once a month. When I was just starting out, I would record an entire month's worth of podcasts on a single day. I booked interviews with experts back to back for that day and got all the recording done at once. The following week, I would block off a day to work on the show notes pages associated with those podcast episodes, as well as the newsletters.

Tanya, one of my students, follows a similar plan: every two weeks she creates scripts for three YouTube episodes and then records them. Another student, Sophia, batches her Instagram content on a two-week schedule, blocking two hours every other week to create her posts.

I know it can feel overwhelming at first to be creating so much content in one go. But I can't tell you how much easier it is to get into a creative state when you don't have any other "job" to do during that time. Your only mandate is to create.

I often find myself looking forward to batch creation days. For me, it's a vast improvement over having to create a new piece of content every single week. When I'm done, I feel so accomplished and liberated!

That said, if you don't want to or can't set aside such a large block of time, you might choose to work on your content during your daily Tiger Time. That's fine too—the goal is simply to find a schedule that works for you and stick with it. And when you're in this dedicated, creative space, make sure to minimize distractions—close any applications on your computer that don't need to be open, or better yet, put your computer in Do Not Disturb mode. Turn off all notifications, put your phone on silent, and if you're at home, make sure whoever is home with you knows not to interrupt you unless absolutely necessary.

Once your content is produced and published, that doesn't mean it's forgotten! After all, creating a really stellar piece of content takes time and love. Rather than thinking of it as one and done, I want you to leverage it so you get as much value out of your effort as possible. The way to do that is to package it up into different shapes and sizes so your audience can consume it in a variety of ways. This is called *repurposing your content*, and it should become part of your ongoing content creation process.

Not sure what I mean by repurposing? Here's an example of how to take one piece of content and quadruple its value—based on what I do for every one of my own podcasts after the recording and editing is complete.

Repurpose #1: Transcribe the audio. Some people prefer to read instead of listen and others might be hard of hearing, so I transcribe the audio from each episode and post it on my website. There are websites and services that do this for a very low cost. In addition to offering the content in multiple forms, the text is full of relevant key words, which gives my website a nice SEO boost.

Repurpose #2: Create quotes and graphics. I read through the content I've transcribed and pull out two or three really good quotes or stats that can be turned into a graphic for use on social media.

Repurpose #3: Give a sneak peek on social media. I'll pull a short audio clip from the original podcast episode to be posted on social media. The same can be done for video. If you're a blogger, you can post a screenshot of a key paragraph from your post.

Repurpose #4: Convert your audio to video. While my favorite platform is the audio podcast, I know my Ideal Customer Avatar also hangs out on YouTube. So I publish my podcasts to YouTube with a static graphic or slide deck. On the other hand, if your primary platform is YouTube, you can just as easily pull the audio from the video and turn it into a podcast episode.

These are just a handful of options—truly, the sky's the limit for how you can take great content and present it in multiple formats. At the same time, when you're just starting out, I encourage you to keep it simple.

If you're producing content only every so often right now, the first thing I want you to work on is consistency—building up to a weekly post that your Ideal Customer Avatar can depend on. Once that habit is in place, you'll start seeing the rewards in terms of your clientele and you'll naturally want to do more. That's when you can go back to the content you've already posted and start repurposing it for other platforms.

The great thing about producing content is that once you get it out there, it can take on a life of its own. So don't wait until all the stars align to start stacking the value for your audience. Start today.

DO THE WORK: CHOOSE A PLATFORM AND PLAN YOUR BATCHING

The time has come to choose your primary content platform and plan your first batch of content. Let's go!

Step One: Choose Your Platform

Review the options I laid out in this chapter, do some research, and talk to your Ideal Customer Avatar. By the end of the week, I want you to make a decision on how you are going to deliver weekly content to your audience.

> **Visit www.twoweeksnoticebook.com/resources for a list of my favorite apps and software for each type of platform.**

Step Two: Plan Your First Batch

Once you know which platform you're going to use to communicate with your audience, I want you to get to work on your first batch planning session. Block out 30 to 60 minutes of uninterrupted time and use these questions to brainstorm content your audience will love:

1. What topics would be beneficial to your Ideal Customer Avatar? What content would enhance their lives?

2. What is your Ideal Customer Avatar struggling with right now?

3. What are some of the questions your Ideal Customer Avatar is already asking you? What are some of the questions they *should* be asking you, but don't know yet?

4. What can you teach your Ideal Customer Avatar or share with them that will inspire, empower, and educate?

5. What myths do you need to dispel?

6. What kind of content will pique their interest and strengthen their desire to learn more from you?

Once you've started creating your weekly content, you'll want to drive traffic toward it. The best way to do that is to email your subscribers each week with a link to your new content. But before you can do that, we need to talk about why an email list is so important and the best way to get it set up—the subject of the next chapter.

Chapter 8

Attract Your Audience
How to Build an Email List

Here we go: yet another cautionary tale from yours truly. This one is about what *absolutely not to do* in your first few years in business. When I was first starting out, it seemed like my attention was going in a million different directions. I had to figure out how to make money to replace my corporate salary. I had to give my clients quality attention so they'd keep coming back. I had to—or so I thought—say yes to every opportunity that came my way. Because, let's be honest, I was feeling desperate.

Amid all this frantic activity, one thing fell to the bottom of the to-do list every single week: working on building my email list. I knew it was an important part of a healthy business in the 21st century, but instead, I nursed a painful case of "shiny object syndrome" and chased opportunities that sounded exciting but did very little to help me build a captivated audience.

Then two years into my journey, I woke up and smelled the Wi-Fi, recognizing that the real opportunity for me would be to sell digital courses online. So I put my heart and soul into building my first course—teaching authors how to launch a book using social media—and was so proud when it was ready. The day my sales page went live I felt like a kid who'd just set up her lemonade stand at the bottom of the driveway, absolutely *sure* I would be a millionaire in no time flat . . . only to get progressively more and more dejected when zero cars drove by over the course of the day.

Slowly the truth dawned: there was no traffic driving by my digital lemonade stand because I had spent *no time* cultivating an audience for said lemonade. I knew there were people out there who needed the information I was offering, but I had no way to get in touch with them! Suddenly I realized my priorities had been exactly the opposite of what they should have been.

This truth was especially hard to swallow, since by that time I'd been working my fingers to the bone for two years. In all the time I'd spent running from one event to the next, handing out condoms—er, fancy metallic business cards—showing up when people asked me to, and doing one-on-one coaching, *I hadn't actually been building my business.*

In today's marketplace, building your business *is* building your email list. Full stop. While I'd managed to support myself, which was a huge win, I hadn't been setting myself up for the future.

Luckily, after that first terrible launch I got with the program and started learning everything I could about building my email list—and my whole business turned around.

ALL HAIL THE MIGHTY EMAIL LIST

So what do I mean by "email list," anyway? I'm simply talking about a list of names and email addresses of your Ideal Customer Avatar who have raised their hand and said they want to hear from you. (If you're wondering where, when, and how to get them to raise their hand, I've got you—we'll be going into all the ways to load up your list in the next chapter.)

Regardless of the platform you've chosen, you're going to need an email list to get that content to the followers who want it most. For this reason, your email list is the single most valuable asset of your business. It's also the measure of the health of your business. Tell me the size, and, more importantly, the engagement levels, of your list, and I can tell you the impact—and revenue—you're making. Why? Because those who invite you into their inboxes are your core fans and by far the group most likely to transition into paying customers.

If you don't have a list or your list is stagnant, it's highly likely your income and your impact will be stagnant too. But when you have an engaged email list, you can make money in your business at any time, as long as you have something of value to offer your subscribers.

Whenever I bring up this concept, I see people get a little uncomfortable. They start to fidget in their seats and their eyes glaze over. They know other priorities are taking their attention away from this all-important effort. They make excuses about why they're not focused on list building. And believe me, I understand! I know it because I lived it. But I want you to really listen to me now: If you slow down for a moment and spend some time setting up a strong list-building foundation, I promise you won't regret it. You'll be putting your business on a trajectory for true momentum and growth.

I'm not exaggerating when I say that the biggest mistake I ever made in my business was waiting almost two years to focus on growing my email list. I'm the first to admit that I've made a *lot* of mistakes, so when I say this was the biggest of them all, I want you to take that seriously. The sooner you start growing your list, the more fans you'll have *forever*.

The people who need and want what you're offering will stay with you for years to come. And not only was I leaving money on the table during those lost years (at a time when I was struggling to make *any* money at all), I also missed out on two years' worth of list-building that I can never get back. If I had been able to see past the shiny objects and focus on making my email list the number one priority, my list would be that much more robust today.

This is why when people ask me when's the best time to start building an email list, I say *yesterday*! But the good news is that the second-best time to start building your list is *today*. So let's make this happen now.

A word of caution before we dive any further into this chapter. If you're reading this thinking, *I've chosen to build my social media following instead of my email list, it's basically the same thing*, then I've got some bad news. While social media can be an incredible tool to help grow your business, it's not enough. You're reading this book because you want to unboss and set yourself up for an amazing future of your own design, right? Well, the hard truth is that social media is not and never will be *yours*.

You don't own the platforms where your followers find and follow you. Building your following on Instagram or TikTok or YouTube is essentially building your business on rented land. It can be useful in the present, but you can get evicted at a moment's notice. The corporations that own the social media sites you depend on can decide to change their algorithms or the rules of the advertising you depend on, and overnight—poof! Your following no longer sees you in their feed.

An email list that *you own* becomes the solid ground that your business is built on. Nobody can take it away from you because you're in control. It's as strong or as weak as you make it, depending on how you cultivate it.

What's more, studies show that email does a better job of turning your Ideal Customer Avatar into a paying customer. While more people may scroll past your product launch on Instagram than will read about it on your list, the list will always convert better.

According to a survey conducted by the Direct Marketing Association (DMA) and Demand Metric, on average, an email list has a return on investment of 122 percent—meaning for every dollar you spend on email marketing, you can make $1.22 in profit. The average ROI of your social media following? One quarter of that.[1] You listening? Email converts four times more effectively than any other digital marketing channel. It's where I want you to be focused because it's where you'll see the most long-term gains.

If you *still* need convincing, take this into account. In the fall of 2021, Facebook and Instagram went dark for almost six hours. That very same day I'd been planning a digital course promotion. If I'd been planning to sell it mostly via social media, I would have been up a creek. Luckily, I was promoting it to just 6 percent of my subscribers. That day I made almost $18,000. With just one email sent to a tiny portion of my list. This is just one reason why, while I love social media as a medium for growth, it can and will never take the place of a quality email list.

QUALITY OVER QUANTITY

Whenever I start talking about email lists, the topic inevitably steers toward numbers. I'll hear things like, "But, Amy, I only have a list of ten people, and five of them are my family!" Or, "I have five thousand people on my list, but when I email them, I hear crickets." Or I get questions like, "How many people should I have on my list?" "What's a 'good' email list size?"

I want to pause right here and make something really clear—when I stress the importance of having an email list, I'm not just talking about the *number* of people who subscribe; I'm talking about the *quality* of those people. Quality is determined by how engaged your subscribers are—whether they're opening your emails, taking action, consuming your weekly content, referring you to other people, and (eventually) purchasing from you. A quality list—one you can count on to convert into sales—is one where you build and maintain a relationship with your subscribers, nurturing that connection and treating them like the VIPs that they are.

And this is where all that content you're creating and releasing weekly to your audience comes into play by adding value to their lives, increasing the "know, like, and trust" factor, and ultimately building loyalty. These relationships will fuel your success, increase your impact, and enable you to grow your business and your bottom line. You do not need a *big* email list to be successful, but you do need an *engaged* email list.

I have so many students who come to me and say, "But, Amy, I only have a few hundred people on my list." I always say the same thing to them: You might not think 100 people is a lot, but invite them over to your house for dinner. If you had 100 people crammed into your dining room, and you were responsible for entertaining them and cooking for them, it would sure feel like a lot! So when you start to get down about your list being too small, remember that each one of those "numbers" is a person that you have the opportunity to impact.

In fact, a few years ago, I did an experiment. And although I have a sizable list (I better if I'm the expert, right?), I decided to test how effective my email marketing strategies would have been if I'd had a smaller list. To do this, I emailed a special offer for a live workshop training for $197 to a small portion of my list, selecting only one thousand people to receive the email. Within 48 hours, we had made more than $6,000. Just like that. Can you imagine the peace of mind you'd have if you knew that at any time you could make $6,000 overnight, just from having a list of one thousand people?

My student Adamaris understands the value of a modest list. She was working as a licensed psychotherapist, but she had big dreams to go out on her own. Not only did she want a business that would allow her to move to another country, she wanted to start her own podcast, host a destination retreat for women, and work with Oprah. No big deal, right? So she quit her job, started her own business, and grew her email list to three hundred people.

By making herself constantly visible to her Ideal Customer Avatar through live video trainings on Facebook, consistently adding value and connecting with new prospects through word-of-mouth and referrals, she took those three hundred people and built a six-figure coaching business giving female entrepreneurs the mindset tools she learned as a psychotherapist. Plus, she launched a podcast, hosted her first retreat, and was featured in *O, the Oprah Magazine*. Talk about a vision board coming to life! She put her goals out into the universe, used what she had—a list of just three hundred people—and every single dream became real.

I hope Adamaris's story helps bust the myth that you need a huge list to do big things. Every email list is small to start. Focus on providing huge value on a regular basis. Engage with your list by emailing them, having conversations with them, and providing solutions to their needs and desires.

In fact, one of my favorite things about having a smaller email list is that you have more opportunity to create personal relationships with your subscribers. When I was starting out, anytime someone wrote in to thank me for a success they had achieved with my content, I would personally reply to their email. If you've ever received a personal note from someone you're following, you know how it can help create customers for life.

Rather than focusing on wishing your number was bigger, think about ways you can personally connect with and customize your messaging to those who have already raised their hand and asked to hear more from you.

SHARE YOUR WEEKLY CONTENT

In order to turn a small list into an *engaged* list, you will need to share content based on their needs and desires. If you deliver free, value-packed content to your subscribers on a consistent schedule, there's no question their loyalty to you and your business will grow.

Once you start creating content every week, start sending it out! Email your list each week with a direct link to your new content. If your content is a blog, you can link directly to the post on your website. If you're producing YouTube videos, you can send your subscribers straight to your YouTube page. If you've created a private community where you host your Q&As, link to the post there. Or send show notes and a link to this week's podcast episode.

In case you're wondering how I alert my list that their weekly *Online Marketing Made Easy* podcast is available, here's an example of a typical email I might send out.

> **Subject Line:** Your guide to planning your pre-launch, webinar, and course content is inside
>
> I've heard your question, **[Name]**! And I've got answers for you.
>
> You know the question . . .

How do I differentiate between prelaunch content, webinar content, and course content without giving it alllll away?!

(Well, if you didn't ask that, trust me when I say many of your peers have!)

This is a fantastic question, **and in today's podcast episode,** I'm giving you crystal-clear guidance on what content should go where and when.

You'll learn . . .

- How to determine **the bulk of your prelaunch content** (and how listening to your audience can help direct you)

- How to leave your audience saying, **"I'm excited! Now, how do I do it?"** on your webinar

- The secrets to creating valuable course content

And so much more!

Take your brilliant entrepreneurial self over to today's episode and get into content creation beast mode. >>>

You'll walk away from today's episode knowing exactly what content you should highlight during your prelaunch phase, your webinar, and what to put in your course. Enjoy!

ALL my best,
Amy

You'll want to make sure to capture your subscribers' attention with your weekly emails, and the best way to do this is with a captivating subject line, followed by an interesting opening paragraph. Notice how I directly addressed the reader by validating them and saying I was going to answer their question? From there you want to use wit, humor, vulnerability, or emotion to pull your reader in. Tell them a story. Maybe ask *them* a question to get them to engage. Just make sure that what you include aligns with your weekly content because that's where you're going to direct them.

Let them know that you have, for example, a new podcast episode that you just created for them—one that can't be missed. Share what they're going to learn, why they should care, why you created it, and what's in it for them. And always make sure that you include a link back to your content.

Don't just copy and paste or share verbatim in your email what you're about to link them to. Your email should be a really compelling teaser, with the ultimate goal to drive traffic to your original piece of weekly content. You want to give your audience a preview of what's to come if they click on the link.

SETTING UP AN EMAIL SERVICE PROVIDER

The three things that my students tell me stand in the way of their willingness to focus on list building are (1) the desire to build a bigger following on social media first, (2) not knowing where to start, and (3) getting overwhelmed by the technology. The good news is, we already debunked roadblock #1—you have no reliable following if you have no email list. As for problems #2 and #3, both are solved almost effortlessly with the help of an email service provider.

An email service provider (ESP, for short) is a tech platform that allows you to collect names and email addresses and then send emails to those contacts easily. While in the early days of Internet marketing, you might have kept your email list in a spreadsheet, cutting and pasting the list into the "BCC" line of the email you were sending, these days list management software is an absolute must-have—not only for ease of use, but because it will ensure you are compliant with current email marketing laws.

Now, I know technology can seem scary. I was personally terrified of ESPs, especially in the beginning when I had no idea what I was doing. (Quite honestly, I'm still not the most technology-proficient gal around!) But because the creators of entry-level ESPs understand that most entrepreneurs aren't tech geniuses, they make using their interface very easy. In fact, one of the hardest parts of setting up your first ESP is wading through the ocean of options that appear when you google *email service provider.*

There are literally dozens and dozens of ESPs out there, each a little different from the next. But ultimately, they all do the same thing: allow you to capture and store email addresses and send emails to the people on your list.

While of course I have my own personal faves (you can find recommendations and comparison guides at www .twoweeksnoticebook.com/resources), deciding which ESP to go with is a very personal decision. Here are a few variables I recommend taking into account:

1. **Price:** Prices vary, with several great options for under $100 per month and pricing going up from there. Some email service providers even offer free versions up to a certain number of contacts.

This may be the right route if you're just getting started, but make sure you're okay with the cost increases down the road after you hit the limit of their free service. Note that many providers offer free trials (typically 14 to 30 days), which is another great way to try out the different options available.

2. **Email Capabilities:** Depending on the needs of your business, both now and down the line, there are certain features that you will want to consider when researching platforms.

   - Does it include automation (i.e., the ability to automatically send a specific sequence of emails based on a number of days since someone subscribed to your list or clicked a link in one of your emails)?

   - Does it include both "broadcast" (a single email) and "campaign" (a sequenced set of emails sent over time) functionalities?

   - Does it allow you to split-test (send two versions of the same email with, for example, different subject lines to see which performs better)?

   - Is there a cap on the number of emails you can send monthly? If so, does this cap work for you?

3. **Templates:** Templates allow even the tech-unsavvy and design-dense among us to both write and format professional looking emails in minutes. They also enable you to create your own custom templates—like a newsletter, with

a particular header and footer—to use again and again.

4. **Additional Capacities:** Does the platform allow you to build landing pages (web pages you can send your audience to, where they can take an action like signing up for your free masterclass or watching a video) and easy-to-use forms for collecting email addresses? Does it offer lead magnet hosting and delivery (the ability to host and send downloadable files)? Can you integrate a shopping cart for e-commerce? Can you create web pages, sales pages, and products?

5. **Support:** How robust is their knowledge base? Do subscription plans come with access to customer service support? Do you have phone support or email only? What are the reviews for the ESP's customer support system?

While this list may have your head spinning, don't fret. Most popular service providers will offer *most* of the functionality you will need. Just remember that what works in the beginning might not be adequate a few years from now. Ideally you'll choose a platform that will grow with you.

While most businesses will switch service providers down the line, the closer a match you can get to what you'll need five years from now, the fewer headaches you'll have to endure.

DON'T COMPARE THE BACK END OF YOUR BUSINESS

Before we move on, we've got to talk about imposter syndrome's pesky stepsister, comparisonitis. You know her.

The one who makes you think, *I'll never have anything as interesting to say as she does. Their graphics are more sophisticated than mine will ever be. He's been making videos for years; I'll never catch up.* Thoughts like these are almost impossible to escape, so instead of avoiding them, it's important to gather the tools you'll need to combat them. Let me set the stage.

It's 11 P.M. and you're burning that entrepreneurial midnight oil, writing your very first email newsletter. You're crafting what you believe is a personal and engaging story to share with your subscribers, and you decide to take a look at a few newsletters in your inbox, just to get a little extra creative push.

You think, *What could it hurt? I'm just looking for a little inspiration!* Next thing you know, you've gone down a never-ending newsletter rabbit hole and your mind is racing with thoughts like, *Oh no. How could I ever compete with that? My newsletter feels like a second grader wrote it! What a joke!* You begin to dig yourself deeper and deeper into that black hole of comparisonitis.

We've all compared ourselves to strangers on the Internet. But that's just it: These people you are obsessing over on the web are *strangers*. And because you don't know them, it's easy to compare the *back end* of your business— the content that's failed to hit the mark, the contractors that didn't live up to their end of the bargain, the mistakes that have been made, the hours spent working on weekends and past bedtimes, the financial uncertainty, all the awkward and dicey aspects of your journey—to the *front end* of theirs.

When you look at someone's witty, creative newsletter or their perfectly curated images on social media, all you see is what they *want* you to see. You have no idea whether things are actually as successful as they seem to be.

As you find your way on your entrepreneurial journey, things are bound to feel messy on your back end. It's normal! But it's not fair for you to compare your messy interior to anyone else's shiny perfect exterior.

We also tend to compare ourselves to people who have been building their businesses for years. For example, you might listen to my podcast *Online Marketing Made Easy* and think, *Amy has it all figured out! She has more than five hundred episodes! I only have 10 episodes!* At that moment you're missing the fact that I started my podcast in 2013. I've been podcasting for many, many years, and there was a time when I, too, had 10 episodes.

Here's my advice: put your head down, get those blinders on, stay in your lane, and just get going. That's how the magic happens.

DO THE WORK: LOOKING AT YOUR LISTS

To get a better understanding of what works and what doesn't when it comes to creating and nurturing an engaged email list, you need look no further than your email inbox. If you're alive at this moment in time, you're subscribed to email lists—probably lots of them. So take a spin over to your inbox and identify three email lists you're on. Do you get a daily email from your favorite retail store? A weekly email from an influencer you follow? A monthly roundup from a resource you use inside your business?

Now identify three different lists you're subscribed to. It's time for a newsletter audit. To do this, I want you to create a Google or Word doc, or if you're old school like me, grab a journal and pen, and get comfy. Create two columns. At the top of one column, write a plus sign. At the top of the other, write a minus sign. Or feel free to use *pro/con, thumbs up/thumbs down,* or whatever works for you!

Next, I want you to spend 30 minutes reviewing at least three emails you've received from each list. As you go through them, I want you to capture the pluses and minuses in your audit document. Things like: What do I like about receiving these emails? What do they do well? Why do I stay on their list? Which parts of these emails do I engage with the most? What makes me click on something? (But remember—the goal here is research, not to get caught up in *comparing* yourself to them.) Now on the other hand: What do I not like about them? What has caused me to consider unsubscribing in the past? What do I wish they could do better? Where are they missing the mark?

Take these ideas and use them to spark creativity for your own email list. Underneath the notes you've taken about what works or doesn't, create a list of five things you want to integrate into your own newsletter. Do you like the way they tell stories? Do you think they overdo it on the gifs and memes? Do they use a more designed, professional look or a more casual feel with just text—and which do you prefer? Do certain subject lines stand out to you that you might emulate?

Alternatively, was there a certain subject line style that you wanted to avoid? Was there a certain structure or certain features to their emails that could work for your business? Was it easy to follow the action they wanted you to take next—like visiting their website, watching a video, or making a purchase?

Write down at least five ways you might take these notes and put them into action. Keep this document somewhere handy so you can pull it out when you start writing your next newsletter.

Now that you understand why a list of engaged email subscribers is your foundation and single most important asset when building an online business, the next step is to start applying strategies that will help you grow your list and develop it into a revenue-generating asset.

Chapter 9

Grow That List!
How to Engage Subscribers with Lead Magnets

Imagine it: You're innocently scrolling on your phone one evening, taking in the day's social media happenings, when suddenly you come across an offer that gives you goose bumps. This is exactly the information you've been waiting for your whole life!

Whether it's a free guide to making gluten-free plant-based dinners in under 30 minutes, a free video training promising step-by-step instructions for setting up your own in-home video studio, or a free audio meditation that guarantees to ease your stress and soothe your anxiety, you know you cannot live without this juicy piece of info. So you click the link, and magically you're transported to a web page where you discover that if only you provide your name and email address, this almost-too-good-to-be-true gift will be quietly delivered to your very own inbox.

If this sounds familiar, then you have personal experience with something called a lead magnet. The "lead" here is, well, *you*! You are the "sales lead," or potential customer, that this amazing piece of content was meant to draw in. The "magnet"—that free resource—made such a powerful promise that you were willing to exchange your valuable email information in order to receive it. And voila: your life is (hopefully) improved by the guide, and the savvy business owner who provided it to you has one more engaged sales lead on their email list.

A lead magnet, sometimes referred to as a freebie or free resource, is the answer to the question "Now that I'm on board with building my email list . . . um, *how*?" It's a free offering that incentivizes potential customers to sign up for your list. You give them something valuable, and they give you their contact information (at minimum their email address, but sometimes their name as well) in exchange.

To create a successful lead magnet, you need to know what your audience wants and needs from you—which requires revisiting your Ideal Customer Avatar from Chapter 5. You also need to have an idea what your paid offering will be, since the ultimate goal of your list is to convert your subscribers into customers for your paid product or service.

Let's say you're a dating coach for introverted women hoping to find "the one." You wouldn't want to grow your list with a lead magnet about how to decorate your house for the holidays or you'd end up with an email list that is a mismatch for the service you're trying to sell.

So when you're thinking about what to include in your first lead magnet, think about this:

- What does your audience need to understand, be aware of, or believe in order to want—or need—your paid product, program, or service down the road?

- And how can you start the conversation with them to meet them where they're at right now?

- Do you need to change their mindset before they're even ready to buy from you?

- Do they need a quick win to get some momentum and a little taste of success?

Take the dating coach example. Perhaps before your core customer would be ready to sign up for a coaching package, she'd need to change her belief that dating is anxiety-producing. In that case, you might create a lead magnet called the Stress-Free Guide to Flirting for Introverts. The goal is for your audience to walk away from your resource saying, "Wow! I can't believe she's giving this away for free!" (BTW: Don't be afraid to give the best stuff away for free! Your paid products will be deeper and more comprehensive—and thus more valuable—than any freebie you might offer.)

Let me share a real-life story of my student Devin. Devin is a financial advisor who simplifies retirement plans for his clients. His free 29-page e-book about how to navigate the social security program wasn't working as a lead magnet because it wasn't something they could skim quickly to gain an understanding of how the program worked.

Devin knew it was too long, so he created a one-page cheat sheet to help his subscribers determine whether they had benefit payments waiting for them. In just 24 hours of promoting his freebie on a Facebook Live video training, he grew his list by 20 percent by gaining more than one thousand new subscribers! That kind of massive adoption and list growth is totally possible for you too.

A FIELD GUIDE TO LEAD MAGNETS

A lead magnet can be essentially *anything* you give your audience for free in exchange for their name and email address. That said, there are a few common varieties that show up again and again, in large part because they *work*! Let's walk through them.

The Cheat Sheet

A cheat sheet is a one- or two-page document that offers a series of steps, guidelines, or examples to help simplify a complex process. Cheat sheets give your customers an overview and basic understanding, saving them the time, energy, and attention it would take to summarize, digest, or memorize the material on their own. It's a resource they can come back to whenever they need a refresher on the topic.

My motto with lead magnets is to make them simple enough that the customer "gets to the finish line" incredibly fast. You don't want it to take weeks for someone to work through the content in your lead magnet. You want them to feel a sense of accomplishment right away and to associate the "win" with your help. A cheat sheet does just that. It's easy to skim, and often has lots of graphics to illustrate the main points, making it simple and digestible. The value is experienced immediately.

I often use cheat sheets inside my courses and in promotional content. For example, I created a 30-day bootcamp to prepare my students for the launch of my Digital Course Academy program. Inside the bootcamp, we reviewed seven key decisions they needed to make in order to create and launch their digital course. At the beginning of the 30 days, I provided attendees with an overview of all seven decisions.

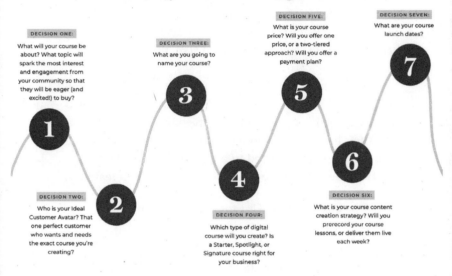

The 7 Key Decisions Planning Guide

DECISION ONE:
What will your course be about? What topic will spark the most interest and engagement from your community so that they will be eager (and excited!) to buy?

DECISION TWO:
Who is your Ideal Customer Avatar? That one perfect customer who wants and needs the exact course you're creating?

DECISION THREE:
What are you going to name your course?

DECISION FOUR:
Which type of digital course will you create? Is a Starter, Spotlight, or Signature course right for your business?

DECISION FIVE:
What is your course price? Will you offer one price, or a two-tiered approach? Will you offer a payment plan?

DECISION SIX:
What is your course content creation strategy? Will you prerecord your course lessons, or deliver them live each week?

DECISION SEVEN:
What are your course launch dates?

Other examples of cheat sheets include:

- Top 5 Metrics Every Business Owner Should Understand

- The Anatomy of a Killer Email Subject Line

- The Best Foods to Pair with Red Wine

- Mastering the Art of the Smoky Eye

- Grandma's Easy Apple Pie Recipe

The Checklist

A checklist is a way for your audience to keep track of their progress toward a goal, ensuring they aren't skipping steps or action items along the way. Checklists are valuable because they help your audience to take action and stay accountable. If they check off each step, they're more likely to get results.

One of my students, Sunny, is a nutritionist. She created a lead magnet called 10 Nutrients Your Thyroid Is Missing. Inside, she included a checklist of 10 nutrients and their benefits to help her students ensure they're getting everything they need to keep their thyroid healthy.

Here are a few more examples to spark your creativity:

- The Ultimate Checklist for Productive Meetings

- 10 Steps to Change a Flat Tire

- Here Comes the Bride: Day-of-Wedding Checklist

- Pantry Staples for Healthy Living Checklist

- The Master Baby Registry Checklist

The Guide

A guide is more robust than a checklist or cheat sheet, providing off-the-charts value for your audience. It often includes a road map to get to a desired outcome, as well as stories and examples to bring the lessons to life. It's key to make your guide highly actionable, to ensure the reader gets results and wants to come back to you for more. But be careful—you don't want your guide to feel like *too* much work, which could prevent them from opening it at all!

One of my students, Jordan, created a guide for coaches and consultants called the VIP Day Road Map. In it, she shares the nine steps to creating and selling a "VIP Day" offer for a full-day meeting or retreat to go deep with a single client. This works well with the more robust "guide" format, because Jordan has a lot to share on this subject.

In addition to walking them through each of the nine steps, Jordan includes how a VIP Day can improve your business and profits, the mistakes to avoid that kill your conversion rates, and more information about who she is and how you can work with her. With a simple cheat sheet, the reader would have missed out on all that additional value.

Some other examples of topics for a guide include:

- A Visitor's Guide to Austin, Texas

- The Beginner's Guide to Web Design

- The Definitive Blueprint to Building a Tree House

- Meditation 101: Quiet Your Mind and Get Focused with 5 Simple Mantras

- Math Curriculum: A Guide for Grades 6–8

The Training

A training gives your audience the opportunity to really get a feel for who you are and how you teach, often in video or audio form, depending on the content and your preference. This kind of lead magnet is more personal, allowing you to get closer to your potential customer and thus create a deeper connection with them. It also helps your audience to see your personality and teaching style and what you're all about; you don't always get that from a PDF guide or cheat sheet.

Financial expert Patrice Washington offers an audio training on *The Truth About Wealth,* where she teaches her audience how to earn more "without chasing money." It's an introduction to Patrice's philosophy and gives you a solid feel for what it would be like to enroll in her paid program.

YouTube is a great resource for examples of video trainings—just be careful not to get lost there for an afternoon! Here are some titles featured on the site:

- How a Costume Designer Creates an Iconic Look

- Lawn Care Tips for Beginners

- Create a Cover Letter That Gets You the Interview

- The Most Common Medical Terms (and How to Say Them in Both English and Español)

- Top 12 Hand Embroidery Stitches

The Mini-Course

To take the training lead magnet one step further, a free mini-course is a *series* of progressive content focused on teaching people about one specific topic. Once a student opts in, you deliver a series of trainings (versus one) via email, most often by video and dripped out over a few days.

A mini-course carries a lot of perceived value. The word *course* shows your audience that you've thoughtfully crafted a framework for delivering the content they need. The word *mini* says that you've also done the hard work of distilling the whole subject into bite-sized pieces that won't feel overwhelming to them.

My dear friend Stu McLaren has a mini-course about how to turn what you already do into a profitable membership program. In exchange for your name and email, he delivers three video trainings. He's offered this lead magnet for several years and has had tens of thousands of opt-ins. Additional examples include:

- Mini Financial Workshop: 4 Steps to Take Before Investing Your Money

- Free Toddler Milestone Mini-Course

- 3-Part Canning Garden Vegetables Series

- The 5 Keys to Fix Your Credit Score Crash Course

- Gaining Confidence in Front of the Camera: A Free Video Series

My only word of caution with mini-courses is to leave your audience wanting more. You don't want them to walk away thinking, *Wow, I just got the full transformation I was hoping to get!* Then they may not feel the need to purchase your product or service, so you need to thread the needle carefully—delivering significant value while leaving them eager for new ways to work with you.

The Challenge

A successful challenge will not only grow your email list quickly, but has the potential to attract new customers and create customers for life. I'm sure you've seen plenty of these out there: *5-Day Sales Funnel Challenge* . . . *7-Day 5K Challenge* . . . *4-Day Book Proposal Writing Challenge.*

A challenge typically lasts 3 to 10 days, and each day you deliver content to your audience encouraging them to take a specific action *that day.* You guide them via daily emails, Zoom calls, or gatherings in a private community like a Facebook group through the different daily challenges to try something new or reach a long-held goal. Since you're showing up day after day, right there with them as they take these bold steps, they get a sense of what it might be like to purchase your product or service.

One of my students, Lauren, wanted to help her audience figure out their own sense of self and style, so she created a one-day challenge called the Love Your Body Style Challenge. She created a private Facebook group just for this challenge, where she hosted a daily live video lesson and provided direct feedback to her audience. She also sent a link to her video lesson via email to anyone who had signed up for the challenge. And she was off-the-charts successful, getting five thousand people to opt in the first time she ran the challenge.

Here are some additional examples of challenges I've seen work well:

- Gain a Social Following in 10 Days

- 14-Day Cost-Cutting Challenge

- 5 Days of Gratitude Journaling

- Closet Cleanout Weekend Challenge

- Reignite Your Marriage in a Week Challenge

Now, before you go off deciding that running a challenge is right for you, I want to be honest: a challenge is not the first lead magnet I would recommend creating. If you're just getting started on the lead magnet journey, I'd encourage you to start with something that's *evergreen*, meaning it's always available for whoever would like it, such as a PDF, video, or audio.

A challenge takes time, strategy, and some experience to put together. It's also time-constrained, meaning it's only available for a limited window. And if you don't get a ton of people joining the challenge, it can feel like a whole lot of work for nothing. But if you want to try something higher risk/higher reward, a successful challenge can make a big impact on your email list and bring a lot of energy to your business.

The Quiz

Offering a fun and insightful quiz is another strategy for building your list. Who doesn't love finding out more about themselves with a quiz? Think about it: We've been doing this since we were 16, taking quizzes in *Cosmopolitan* magazine to find out what our favorite Halloween candy says about our relationship status. And now we've upgraded to Buzzfeed, where we can find out which celebrity dog we resemble or which Hogwarts house we would be in. People *love* quizzes.

If you're intentional about creating a quiz for your audience, they can actually provide real value—teaching your audience something about themselves that they didn't already know. Based on the outcome, you can provide specific guidance and resources for exactly where they are as it relates to your area of expertise. If your quiz works, the outcome will resonate with the quiz taker—"She really gets me!"—and also guide them to success in the next step.

When they get their quiz results, you can offer them resources tailored to exactly what they need right now. Done right, a quiz can help your audience get a glimpse of the solution to their problem and a visceral sense of how helpful you can be—which eventually leads them to your product or service.

I've used a quiz to promote my signature course, Digital Course Academy, for several years. I've tried different quiz topics along the way, everything from Are You Ready for a Digital Course? to What's Your Personal Path to Creating a Profitable Digital Course?

Let's check out some additional examples from some of my students and colleagues:

- Discover Your Digital Dream Job

- Is Your Child Safe in Their Car Seat?

- Are You Ready to Sell Your Home?

- Do You Have Good Work-Life Balance?

And my personal favorite . . .

- What Type of Quiz Should You Create for Your Online Biz?

The Email Newsletter

There's nothing more "intimate" in the online space than your inbox. Different from the weekly email newsletters that direct your entire email list to your weekly content, an email newsletter lead magnet delivers "never before seen" content that is created for a specific group of subscribers only, the exclusivity of which increases the perceived value of what you are providing. It's not a one-and-done experience for your subscriber. Instead it's a continued relationship, where you get to engage and connect with your reader on an ongoing basis.

The parenting blog Lucie's List offers an example of an email newsletter. Appropriately named "Crib Sheet," this newsletter requires you to enter your child's age or expected due date upon opt-in, after which you receive content tailored to exactly what you're dealing with in that moment, whether that's upcoming physical changes you can expect based on your pregnancy trimester or the kind of gear your child needs at one year versus two.

Here's a list of some other popular email newsletter topics:

- Top 5 News Stories of the Week

- 10 Best Articles This Month on Digital Marketing

- 50 Things to Do This Weekend

- Seasonal Recipes in 30 Minutes or Less

- 3 Self-Improvement Tips to Boost Productivity

Text Messages

Almost everyone has a mobile device and sends and receives text messages, which means text messages get opened. Text messaging allows you to communicate with your audience in a personal and conversational way. It's highly accessible, likely to be seen, and can be kept short and simple.

If you're looking to deliver short-form content, like a daily reminder or tip, this platform can work really well. Just remember to be mindful of the frequency and content of your messages to limit opt-outs. I highly recommend using text messaging software in order to collect phone numbers and send texts rather than trying to do it manually. This will ease the burden on you as your audience grows and will keep you in compliance with communication regulations. It also might help to communicate up front how often those that sign up to receive texts can expect to hear from you.

Entrepreneur and marketing expert Gary Vaynerchuk sends text messages to his community, and even separates his messages into different groups, organized by hashtags. As a user, all you have to do is text the hashtags of the groups you want to be a part of to a specific phone number, and you've opted in to all the messages for those subjects. He has groups like #AskGaryVee, #Twitter, #Podcast, as well as #wine and #NBA.

For additional text message ideas, check out these sample themes:

- Get Your Questions Answered with a Customer Support Rep

- Daily Mindfulness Tips

- Stay in Touch with Personal Messages

- Order Updates for Physical Products

- Weekly Song Choice to Stay in the Flow

LEAD MAGNET DELIVERY

The above list of lead magnets represents just a few of the dozens of ways to create a lead magnet. You could also create an eBook or design template, write a report or whitepaper, create a calculator, put together case studies, offer a free trial, or provide a coupon or discount for your product or service. The possibilities are endless. Just remember that the goal is to attract quality leads, meaning people who would be a good fit for your product or services. Do this by creating content that will walk them from wherever they are now to the point where your paid offer would be the logical next step.

Once you've created your lead magnet, it's time to design a web page where your leads will give you their email address in exchange for your valuable content. Remember back at the beginning of the chapter, when you were scrolling through social media and got stopped in your tracks by an offer you couldn't refuse? You then clicked the link and were whisked off to a web page that contained a form, asking for your name and email address. This page is called an *opt-in page*—appropriately named, since this is where your potential new subscribers will opt into your email list.

Most website platforms and some ESPs make opt-in pages very simple to create, with drag-and-drop templates and forms that make it easy to get up and running quickly. In addition to your opt-in page, you'll want to create what's called a "thank-you page," which is where the subscriber lands after clicking the "submit" button on the opt-in page. It usually says—get ready for this—*thank you*! It also reminds them that their free gift is waiting in their email inbox. In certain cases such as the first video of a mini-course, the freebie may appear right there on the thank-you page.

Most high-converting opt-in pages follow specific norms around content, layout, registration, and thank-you pages. And of course, the opt-in page should directly connect with your email software, capturing the registration details so the lead becomes part of your ongoing email list. Since you can't be too detailed, let me walk through each of these norms in turn.

Opt-In Page Offer

When future subscribers click the button or link to access your lead magnet, they will land on the opt-in page. Here, you have a chance to further encourage them to provide their contact info in exchange for the lead magnet. This encouragement is called the "opt-in page offer," and it's marketing copy when you get right down to it. So it needs to be clear, focused, and relevant.

Make sure you define the pain point your audience is feeling and how your lead magnet provides the solution or benefit they'll get if they read/watch/listen to it. Avoid going overboard with too much information. There are really only two relevant details to highlight about your lead magnet: (1) it provides results, and (2) it's free.

Here's an example of the copy I used on an opt-in page for a lead magnet I created at the start of the COVID-19 pandemic:

FREE PDF DOWNLOAD

How To Be Productive Working From Home During Uncertainty

Your condensed guide to work-from-home success! Whether you're new to working from home, or you're a remote work pro, these tips will help you to be happier, more productive, and more effective in your new workplace. This guide includes ways that you can support your community — without ever leaving your home — and tools for keeping an abundance mindset.

GET IT NOW!

Opt-In Page Layout

The opt-in page layout should follow a simple flow that leads your audience to take the specific action you want them to take (e.g., "click the GET IT NOW button"). Don't clutter up this page with links to your home page or blog; make sure there is only one call to action available.

Whether your opt-in page is a new page on your website or lives inside your email service provider, you'll want to make sure it aligns with your branding. It's up to you to change the colors, fonts, logos, and other design elements so it feels like a seamless transition from your main site. Offering your potential clients consistent branding helps keep them in the flow of their customer journey, so it's worth paying attention to!

Opt-In Page Registration Process

The registration process should include an easy-to-navigate form to capture the lead's contact information. This is the information you're collecting in exchange for the lead magnet, and the key is to make it simple for your audience to give it to you. The less you ask for, the more likely someone is to sign up. Unless you truly need a last name, mailing address, or phone number, I suggest only using two registration fields: first name and email address.

For my work-from-home lead magnet, my opt-in page had only one action: click the "GET IT NOW" button. Once someone took the action, the following pop-up box appeared:

Grab your guide that contains everything you need to know to work remote successfully.

First Name

Email

YES PLEASE!

Thank-You Page

After you've set up your opt-in page, you'll want to create a thank-you page that will pop up upon successful submission. It's always nice when you sign up for something to get confirmation that your contact information went through. Plus, your thank-you page is the place to give your new subscribers their "next steps" for where to go and what to do to access the lead magnet you promised them.

Here's the copy for the thank-you my subscribers received when they signed up for my free guide on how to work from home:

THANK YOU FOR SIGNING UP

Check your inbox to grab your freebie... Now let's get to work!

No email? Be sure to check your spam folder. You can contact us at **support@amyporterfield.com** if you need additional assistance.

Integrate with Your Email Service Provider

It's time to get everything connected! Once your opt-in and thank-you pages are ready to go, you'll want to make sure they're integrated with your email software. You may have created these pages within your email service provider's system, and if so, nothing else needs to be done. But if you created these pages in WordPress or a different software, then you need to follow your ESP's instructions for connecting the fields on your web page with your ESP database. Once you're connected, you'll be able to easily email your leads with your weekly content—over time turning them from a lead to a customer.

LEAD MAGNET PROMOTION

In order for your lead magnet to do its job, people need to know it exists. My student Rose started mentioning her lead magnet in her YouTube videos, and once her channel took off, she saw her email list explode to over 15 thousand people in just one month. So call attention to your new resource whenever and wherever your potential customers might be: link to it in your social media bios, mention it in your weekly content, link to it from your website, and share it when you do video and podcast interviews. (We'll dive into this in the next chapter.) When you're ready for it, you can also use paid advertising to drive traffic to your opt-in page.

I know this part can feel scary! In fact, about two months into building my own business, I created my first guide about how to get more followers on Facebook, but I was incredibly hesitant to let people know it existed. Hobie asked me what was stopping me, and I knew right away: I was afraid of what my former co-workers—not to mention my former boss Tony Robbins—would think of me. *Who is she to be building her own business? She doesn't know enough. She's not ready.* As I shared my deep insecurities with Hobie, he looked at me sweetly.

"Babe?" he said. "I need to tell you something. Your former co-workers, and specifically Tony, well . . . how do I say this nicely? They are not thinking about you at all. I hate to break it to you, but they are focused on their own stuff. They have other things going on." I was instantly hit with a wave of embarrassment, realizing I was thinking the whole world revolved around me. But then I felt relieved: Hobie was right. They were all focused on their own businesses, in their own worlds. I was no longer part of that equation.

When you think about creating your lead magnet and putting it out there for the world to see and consume, you might find yourself stalling for the same reasons I was. *What will they think?* is a question that pops into every entrepreneur's mind as they begin to post online. But remember, your family, co-workers, former bosses, and strangers online—because, yeah, no matter how silly it sounds, we sometimes worry what complete strangers on the Internet will think!—are all busy doing their own thing. (Probably worrying what *you* will think about whatever they're up to!) And so what if they *do* think you're nuts or not ready or whatever you're afraid of? In that case, just remember Jasmine's words of wisdom: "You're not for everyone, boo."

*　*　*

Before I wrap this chapter up, I want to share one more story about the power of a good lead magnet. After working in the digital marketing field for six years, Eva took the leap and went out on her own as a consultant. She finally experienced the free time she'd been craving for so long, and she started to do some serious soul-searching, releasing unconscious beliefs and old patterns that had been holding her back.

The transformation she experienced was so life-changing that she eventually decided she wanted to shift her consulting focus away from digital marketing toward teaching others the inner work that had helped her so much. The problem? She didn't have an audience for this new industry.

No stranger to entrepreneurship, Eva set up a completely new website and lead magnet to help her audience overcome the resistance that kept them from meditating and started creating weekly content. Three months after one appearance on a colleague's podcast where she mentioned her new lead magnet, she grew her email list from 125 people to over 1,000. Never underestimate the power of a good lead magnet!

DO THE WORK: DESIGN YOUR LEAD MAGNET

Now it's time for you to choose which *type* of lead magnet you're going to create. Will it be a PDF checklist? Three-part video course? Personality quiz? Once you've made that decision, you can start dreaming up ideas for what the *content* of the lead magnet will be.

Remember, you want to create something your audience can't resist, something enticing enough that they'll be willing to exchange their precious email address to get it. Use these questions to help fuel your creativity:

- What is the best place to start the conversation with your Ideal Customer Avatar?

- What is the number one question you get asked all the time?

- What is your Ideal Customer Avatar most afraid of?

- What could help your Ideal Customer Avatar right this minute?

- What is something your Ideal Customer Avatar is not expecting from you, yet if you offered it for free, it would knock their socks off? (Think quick wins—nothing too lengthy!)

- What does your Ideal Customer Avatar need to believe about themselves or about their situation before they buy your product or service?

- How can you get your Ideal Customer Avatar unstuck or out of overwhelm?

- What are your Ideal Customer Avatar's biggest pain points and/or desires? What would help ease their pain or help fulfill those desires?

- What content would be so valuable that your Ideal Customer Avatar would say, "I can't believe this is free!"

Now, in your journal or on the device of your choice, fill out the following worksheet:

Lead Magnet Title:

_____

Lead Magnet Outcome / Transformation *(i.e., What is the benefit your Ideal Customer Avatar will get once they go through your lead magnet?):*

_____

_____

_____

_____

_____

_____

Top 3-5 Content Points *(i.e., Using the previous questions, what are the top 3–5 pieces of content you will include in your lead magnet?):*

_____

_____

_____

_____

_____

_____

_____

_____

3 To-Dos to Create Lead Magnet *(i.e., What are three actions you will take right away to get this lead magnet created?):*

_____

_____

_____

_____

_____

_____

_____

Deadline *(i.e., When will you have this lead magnet created and ready to share with the world?):*

_____

_____

So now that you're ready to get your lead magnet out there, it's time to start promoting it and engaging with your audience—by leveraging perhaps the most useful, and challenging, area for today's entrepreneur: social media.

Chapter 10

Make Social Media Work for You
How to Build a Following on Your Terms

For 13 years, Jamie worked in accounting for a big beverage bottler. On paper it was a great gig. She enjoyed it, and, even better, she was good at it. But every day she would wake up, put in her hours, scramble to get dinner on the table and put her kids to bed, and then wake up and do it all over again. She felt beholden to everyone's agenda but her own, without any control over her own time and missing a sense of freedom.

Although Jamie enjoyed the recognition she got in corporate because she was an achiever by nature, she knew she wanted to do something that had an impact on the world in a way her current job did not. In fact, she would look at the successful women in her industry and think, *That is not the life I want for myself and my family.* She knew she wasn't willing to give up everything she saw these women giving up in order to get to where they were.

It wasn't until Jamie was eight months pregnant with her second child, working long hours on a multibillion-dollar merger that would soon put her out of a job, that something clicked. Taking her severance, she moved her family back to her hometown while she tried to figure out her next steps.

Having never been outside the traditional corporate world, she wasn't sure how to make money without working for someone else. And now being a mom of two, she was struggling to follow her heart to pursue the career she wanted while still providing for her family. But in the meantime, she started taking on clients, consulting on typical, run-of-the-mill accounting and finance services.

Most of her clients were women, and the longer she worked with them, the more she saw a gap in the marketplace—one that she knew she had the ability to fill. Women wanted to learn about finances from other women, but the financial consulting industry was traditionally male dominated.

In response, Jamie turned to social media. She created a Facebook group called Financial Literacy for Women Business Owners and started showing up live every week. She directed the women in the group to her email list by offering a lead magnet guide called "The 7 Finance Pitfalls to Avoid for Solopreneurs." In just a month and a half, she generated a following of more than 1,200 members, with 400 people on her email list and a fully booked client schedule.

When the COVID pandemic hit, Jamie went live almost daily in her group, answering questions and diving into the confusing world of stimulus checks and PPP loans. She was gaining followers by the thousands, with members asking to Venmo her compensation for all the free advice she was giving. Instead, she created a crash course called "Financial Fitness Basics," which generated more than six figures in just two weeks. Jamie realized that by leveraging the power of social media, she was able to build a business on her own, support her family, and help thousands of women in the process.

You've seen the stats. More than 50 percent of the total global population uses social media. Almost half a billion new users are joining each year, and 90 percent of millennials—the largest adult population in the United States—interact with these platforms on a daily basis.

And it's not just the sheer numbers of those engaging, but the amount of *time* they are engaged that matters. People spend more than two hours *each day*, or roughly 15 to 20 percent of their waking lives, on social media. If you add up all the time spent by every user in a day, it's more than 10 billion hours, which equals almost 1.2 million years.[1] In one *day*!

Clearly, social media offers an incredible opportunity as a business owner to make an impact on the life of your Ideal Customer Avatar. It allows you to connect with your audience directly and reach more people than ever before—helping you build relationships that could not have existed two decades ago. It also gives you a way to attract new customers and create brand awareness.

With search functions, hashtags, tagging options, and social sharing, it's easier than ever for people to find *you* and what you have to offer. And while I believe wholeheartedly that social media should never take the place of a quality email list, there are few resources out there so powerful when it comes to *growing* your email list. The connections you create via social media are gold when it comes to promoting and delivering all the hard work you've undertaken—from helping your Ideal Customer Avatar find and click your "subscribe" button to consuming all the valuable content you've been creating.

That said, before we get too far down the "social media is magic" path, we need to pause to acknowledge the other side of the coin. There's really no denying that social media, while amazing in some ways, is a dumpster fire in others. From wasted time (how many times have you found yourself mindlessly scrolling for hours on end?) to comparisonitis (I don't know about you, but I rarely get off Instagram feeling great about myself) to red herrings (how many unnecessary business pivots have I made just because I saw so-and-so doing it on Facebook?).

And that's only the entrepreneurial side of things. Much more serious issues have been linked to social media recently, including online bullying, body image issues, anxiety, depression, and other mental health challenges. Sometimes it feels like social media is more of a curse than a blessing.

Given these issues, as a new business owner, how can you leverage the benefits of social media to grow your business, build genuine relationships, and generate revenue, all while avoiding and not contributing to its downsides? In other words, how can you do social media on your own terms?

ON YOUR OWN TERMS

I'll be honest: For years I had a constant internal battle with social media. I found myself constantly comparing myself to others and envying the people who were willing to put themselves out there, be silly, experiment, and have fun. When I would try it for myself, it always felt forced and awkward.

But since I knew that an engaged social media presence could grow my audience, strengthen my relationship to my community, and ultimately lead to more impact and sales, I made a commitment to myself that I would post something, *anything*, on Instagram for 30 days straight.

I've always loved a good challenge, and this seemed like a fun way to break through my own internal mindset blocks and do something to help my business in the process.

It was only one month—a short enough length of time that I couldn't make excuses to get out of it, but long enough to force me out of my comfort zone and hope-fully to form a habit (they say it takes 21 days to form a habit, right?). So off I went on my personal challenge, cre-ating content to help my students, designing posts I hoped would encourage engagement, and of course including some photos of my dog, Scout.

I didn't quite make my goal—I ended up skipping a day here and there—but the consistent and repetitive action and exposure was enough. I got more comfortable being seen and started to look forward to engaging with my followers. And as a bonus, I gained some important insight into what was resonating with my audience—and what wasn't. The days when my posts didn't land were the days I'd fallen back into my old people-pleasing patterns, fearful to put myself out there and not be accepted. But when I would show up as myself, *my* people responded. (Scout, yes. Photos of me from professional photoshoots, not so much.) A great reminder that I'm not for everyone, and that's okay.

Ultimately, we have to learn to manage our relation-ship with social media, listen to our gut, and stay true to ourselves and our business. What that means will be dif-ferent for each and every person. The goal is to figure out what that looks like for *you*.

You can do video if that's what floats your boat, or you can post beautiful photos or inspiring quotes. You don't need to master the latest TikTok craze or try out every YouTube trend that comes along—but I do think it's important to be brave and try new things.

For example, my student Tracy uses Facebook's birthday feature to send personalized birthday messages to her audience. Sophia uses Instagram Reels as a way to do something fun with her kids and to give her audience a glimpse of what her life is like behind the scenes. Amanda has seen viewership increase after making a point to use relevant hashtags. Gina gets into her direct messages and reaches out individually to potential customers. Just start experimenting and see what works for you!

At the same time, it's key to find the sweet spot between what resonates with your Ideal Customer Avatar and what feels aligned with your values as a business owner. For example, I get feedback *all the time* from followers who say that they want to see an unpolished version of me— no makeup, in my sweatpants, baring it all. But while I run what some people might consider a personality-based business, my product is still a *business* product. So for me, showing up in my pj's for a Facebook Live feels unprofessional and off-brand—totally not "me."

Authentic Amy *is* looking professional and put-together! To me, putting my true self out there means recording a podcast episode where I talk about my pain points in my business, or how I've battled depression and anxiety, or my longtime struggle with my body. While it's true that "real," "raw," "authentic" sharing gets more engagement, you get to decide what that means for *you*.

If you need more inspiration on how to start putting yourself out there on social media, try your own challenge. Commit to posting something on one platform of your choice (ideally one where your Ideal Customer Avatar likes to hang out) for 30 days. Or try a different avenue and promise yourself you'll at least *create* one piece of postable content every day, whether you post it or not.

My social media manager recently challenged me to do this. I had to take one photo every day of something happening in my life—working at my desk, recording a podcast episode, sitting outside with my coffee, walking Scout, going on a date night with Hobie—and send it to her. We didn't post every photo right away, but after 30 days, we had a library of content that served us in the months that followed.

You don't need a team of people to do this; just commit to taking a photo and start saying cheese! The goal is to create a ritual—a consistent habit of showing up, showing your face, and sharing your thoughts—that brings your community more deeply into your life and makes you feel like a part of *theirs*.

Keep in mind, even after you've committed to your 30 days, that doesn't mean you will suddenly see the same success that your favorite influencer is seeing. As Jen Atkin (named the "Most Influential Hairstylist in the World" by *The New York Times*) puts it so perfectly in her book *Blowing My Way to the Top*, "As long as you're making strides toward your goal, whatever that may be, don't get frustrated about how long it's taking. It takes *everyone* a while, but most people don't post about the slog because it's more interesting to share the milestones than the grunt work."

I want to remind you what we talked about in Chapter 8—avoid comparing your back end to someone else's front end. What gets posted on social media is often the highlight reel of someone's best days. It's the end product; you don't see the hours, weeks, and *years* of hard work that got them there in the first place. Success does not happen overnight, even though the Internet might make it seem that way. Social media can create a sense of false urgency inside all of us—but it's *false*. Just keep moving forward and stay committed, and your hard work will pay off.

Rather than comparing yourself, I suggest you use your scrolling time to become a detective. Think about the social media sites you absolutely love, the accounts you follow, the brands and people you trust.

- Why do you think these accounts are so captivating?

- What is it specifically that you love?

- Are they polished or more informal and casual?

- Do they share a lot of "behind-the-scenes" content?

- Do they tell stories about their clients or share about their own personal lives?

- Are they offering you services or products you can purchase, or are they sharing free information?

- What about the way they communicate could you model in your own social media strategy?

- Which strategies seem to be working, and how might you integrate them into your business?

Just as with your email list, I want you to focus on quality over quantity here. When it comes to social media, the measure of quality is *engagement*. What that means is that you're looking for followers who want what you're offering—which they'll let you know by liking, sharing, and commenting on your posts.

In other words, the goal is not to get a million random people to click the "follow" button. If your followers aren't your Ideal Customer Avatar, they're unlikely to engage with you again. I'd rather you make direct connections and build lifelong relationships with a smaller number of people than have millions of followers who scroll right by.

The way to foster this kind of deeper connection is to engage directly with those who are engaging with you. Reply to their comments, turn their questions into future posts, and encourage conversations. A lasting relationship with one client is worth more to your business than 10 thousand followers who never give you the time of day. Start by showering a small but loyal audience with attention and watch your impact grow over time. The best way to do this? By stepping outside of our insecurities and showing up as *ourselves*—authentically and unapologetically.

CREATE YOUR CONTENT PILLARS

As with any communication you make to your audience, when it comes to social media, consistency is key. But I know the next question you're probably wondering is, *How the heck do I know what to post, and how often should I really be posting?*

Let me share a strategy I use in my own business to keep myself organized and the content ideas flowing. You want to show your audience that they can depend on you and that you will show up for them, rain or shine. Because as renowned speaker and salesman Zig Ziglar said, "If people like you, they'll listen to you, but if they trust you they'll do business with you."

I always suggest that you should aim to post at least three to five times a week. If you can post daily, that's even better. Start where you can really commit and stay consistent. Chances are as you keep posting and see the engagement grow, you'll start to enjoy it and will naturally want to increase your frequency.

As for *what* to post, I recommend creating a set of content pillars for all your social content. A content pillar is a specific category of content that you post consistently each week. For example, here's my typical social media plan:

- **Monday:** Instagram Reel (short-form video)

- **Tuesday:** Infographic

- **Wednesday:** Something lifestyle or personal (any format)

- **Thursday:** Promote my long-form podcast episode (which is released every Thursday)

- **Friday:** A quote graphic

- **Saturday/Sunday:** Something personal (any format)

Typically the topic featured in my weekly long-form podcast episode is what drives the theme for the other days of content. For example, the week I released my podcast episode #388: "A Behind-the-Scenes Look into the Habits Successful Entrepreneurs Live By," my daily social content looked like this:

- **Sunday:** Post with a video of Scout (I told you, my audience loves a good pup shot!)

- **Monday:** Instagram Reel on what true freedom in your life looks like and why habits can help you achieve it

- **Tuesday:** Infographic about morning routine dos and don'ts

- **Wednesday:** Instagram Story of the six daily habits I swear by

- **Thursday:** Post and Instagram Story about podcast episode

- **Friday:** A quote graphic pulled directly from the podcast episode

- **Saturday:** A post with a quote about taking small daily action

As you can see, sometimes the pillar is simply the "format" of the content I'm committing to post that day (video, quote graphic, infographic) and sometimes it names the "theme" I'll be posting about (here the theme was habit formation). Now before your head explodes at the sheer quantity of what I post, please remember *I have been doing this for many years at this point*. My business has already launched and has been growing for more than a decade. I also have a team working with me, which means I have a lot of support in both the content creation and the posting.

Was I posting this much when I first went out on my own? Heck no! And do I expect you to have the time and skill to roll out a week like this one *today*? Nope. Not at all.

Instead, I want you to choose at least two to three days where you'll commit to sharing a specific pillar, and commit to doing so for the next month. You can do anything for a month, right? Plus, this starting place will teach you so much about what you love posting, what you never want to post again, and what your audience wants to hear from you. It will be a really useful learning experience, I promise!

So let's get started. Choose two or three of the pillars from the chart below (to mix it up, try to choose at least one from the "format" column and one from the "theme" column) and schedule them in your calendar to post over the next month. Then schedule a 30-minute batch planning session to map out the topics you want to share on, as well as time to batch the content. Schedule it to make it real, and you'll be shocked how quickly you'll find your own social media groove.

Format Pillars	Theme Pillars
Video clip	Promote your weekly content
Audio clip	Goals for the week/day
Infographic	Biggest takeaways from the week/day
Image/photograph	Thought-provoking quotes
Q&A or engagement question	Sources of inspiration
Blog post	Behind the scenes
Text-based graphic	Favorite item (book, product, brand, other social media account, etc.)

AUTOMATING CONTENT

Back when I was starting to post on social media, I slogged through the "posting" process on every single platform. I would overthink every photo and every caption, trying to look and sound "better" than the real me. I also thought that every one of the influencers I followed must be on Instagram 24/7 since they were posting so frequently. I didn't know they had a secret—one I'm officially letting you in on!

Nobody is posting manually multiple times a day, or even multiple times per week. Instead, all those accounts you follow and love are using scheduling software that allows you to upload your content to automatically push out on the schedule you choose. This means you can batch, create, and upload your posts once a week (or if you're the super-organized type, once a month!) rather than having to make time to upload content on a daily basis.

There are many social media management platforms that let you schedule social content in advance, and you can find a full breakdown of my current favorites at www .twoweeksnoticebook.com/resources. Free platforms typically offer plans that handle the daily scheduling tasks and allow you to manage social media activity across all your accounts in one place. (Even though I recommend starting with just one social platform, I want you to be able to scale up to multiple social sites once you're ready to do so.)

As you hit your stride or maybe have a team of your own, you may want to upgrade to a paid service tier that will allow for more advanced options like multiple users and reporting on post performance so you can see what's hitting the mark and what's not. Whether you use a free or paid service, be sure to look for a management tool that allows you to schedule ahead and supports a consistent social media presence across multiple platforms, so it ultimately makes your life easier.

DO THE WORK: CHOOSE YOUR PLATFORM

Right now I want you to focus on choosing the one platform that makes the most sense for your business. As you grow, you'll be able to repurpose content across platforms. To see which is the right fit for your business, I've made an overview of the major platforms and what I suggest posting there.

	Demographic	What to Post
Facebook	Slightly older (mostly between the ages of 25 to 55). An online community around your "you" factor or a collaborative group environment.	Facebook Lives and interactive content like polls and requests for recommendations. The more engaging and interactive the content is, the better it will do.
Instagram	Slightly younger (mostly between the ages of 18 to 34). More informal and personal.	Stunning visual imagery and design, as well as videos (both short form and long form).
LinkedIn	The "professional" space, including fellow business owners.	Original content to build your authority. Long-form copy like blog posts, native content (written in the site, rather than links to external sites), and top 10 lists.
Pinterest	Adult women.	Content to drive traffic to your website since there's no like/comment functionality. Appealing photos of your products, infographics about your area of expertise, or highly designed teasers for your weekly content.

	Demographic	What to Post
YouTube	All ages and gender identities.	Long- or short-form video, including instructional content, tutorials, product reviews, "best of" lists, Q&As, interviews, and everything in between. SEO-friendly content since YouTube is one of the top Internet search engines.
Twitter	Adult males, aged 25 to 50.	Short-form, text-based content, including news updates, trending information, and links to longer-form content like articles and videos.
TikTok	Largely on the younger side (10 to 34), but a growing older audience (35 to 54).	Catchy and trendy short-form videos of up to three minutes, using filters, music, and on-screen graphics to tell engaging stories, be upbeat, and have fun.

Now take a moment to refresh your memory on your Ideal Customer Avatar from Chapter 5:

- Where does your Ideal Customer Avatar already hang out online?

- Are there any specific demographics about your Ideal Customer Avatar that align more closely with one platform over another?

- What is your primary objective with social media? In other words, are you looking to increase brand awareness, connect and engage with your audience, drive traffic to your website, increase your authority as an expert, etc.?

- What content type is best suited for your strengths? Are you comfortable on live video? Are you a great writer? Do you have an eye for beautiful visuals?

Based on your answers, choose the most relevant platform. Make an account if you don't have one already. Then map out two to three weekly content pillars and outline what your posts will look like for the next few weeks. Or if you're like me and have some reservations, give yourself a challenge that will push you a little outside of your comfort zone but is still attainable.

And remember—always keep your Ideal Customer Avatar in mind, stay true to yourself, and trust your gut. The whole point of unbossing yourself and creating your own business is so you have the freedom to do things *your* way—and how you do social media is no exception.

Over the last 10 chapters, I've armed you with the steps you need to get your business up and running. Now it's time to start talking about how to actually make money in your business by leveraging one of three revenue-generating strategies.

Chapter 11

Let's Go Make Some Money
Three Revenue-Generating Strategies

I love a good background story, even when it's a cringey one. So let's travel back in time to one of my first launches. It was early on in my career as an entrepreneur, and I didn't have any step-by-step guidance, so I was figuring it out on my own by trial and error—and let's be honest, mostly by error.

I was committed to doing all the launch things I'd heard about online. I hired someone to help me build a sales page, wrote all my emails in advance, and scheduled my social posts. I expected big things, and big money. I had spent thousands of dollars, left behind a stable career, and worked tirelessly for this moment.

In the end, I walked away with $267 in profit. Yikes!

At the very top of the list of errors was the topic of the course itself. I was overwhelmed by all the advice I was getting online about how to choose which course to teach. I knew it needed to be about social media, since that was my specialty at the time. But I was also hearing that it's important to pick a narrow topic and target a very specific audience. It was getting down to the wire and I was panicking. By the time someone suggested I teach about how to launch a book using social media, I was so relieved to have a topic—any topic—that I just ran with it.

The only problem? I had never launched a book before—much less taught *others* how to do it. (While I am adamant that you don't need to be a certified expert in order to provide value to your audience—you just need that 10 percent edge we talked about in Chapter 4—it does help to have *some* experience in what you're trying to teach!)

Up second in terms of errors was that I hadn't taken the time to do all the things I just walked you through in Chapters 7 and 8. I hadn't put time and attention on creating an engaged audience prior to launching, and I hadn't been communicating with my small list of subscribers regularly to prepare them for this course. In other words, I asked a bunch of people who hardly knew me to give me their money without first giving them evidence that I knew what I was talking about. Looking back, I wonder how I even made that $267!

I felt like the biggest failure of all time. So naturally, I threw myself a pity party. I stayed in bed, mortified at the thought of facing the real world. I moped around in my worn-out black robe for days. I felt like everything I had been building had come crashing down around me.

It's hard for me to admit this because I'd like to say I was able to bounce back quickly on my own, but it took two external sources to get my head back in the game. The first was Hobie. Always my biggest cheerleader, and also likely scared I would never get out of that black robe, he told me in the most encouraging way possible to "get up, get dressed, and keep going."

Hearing that snapped me out of my daze. I realized I was making the launch failure mean that *I* was a failure. I was hinging my entire worth as an entrepreneur on one plan that didn't go as planned—and deciding that I must not be cut out to be a business owner after all. Instead of focusing on where I went wrong, I needed to get clear on what I wanted: What topic *could* I teach effectively? What projects would light me up? And what was my next best move?

I didn't need to look for perfection, but rather for progress. Hearing those encouraging words from Hobie reminded me that I was in this for the long haul. I knew I couldn't go back to having a boss. I also knew I had to keep believing in myself and what I could do.

The second wake-up call came a few days later, when I managed to drag myself to a business mastermind I was a part of. I showed up bloodied and bruised. I had taken the turnout of my launch very hard and brought that attitude and energy with me to the group. I could barely talk without crying, and I didn't engage with the group at all. The mastermind was full of women who seemed like they were already so much further along than me, and because of my launch, I felt embarrassed to even look them in the eye.

But luckily, one of the women in the group who had become a mentor to me pulled me aside.

"I know you're upset, but you have to get back in the game," she told me. "You've got to ask yourself, 'What did I learn? What am I going to do differently next time?'"

Hearing this wasn't easy, trust me. But it was my second wake-up call. This was my first really big failure, and it certainly wasn't going to be my last. I couldn't freak out every single time something didn't go right or I'd be wearing the black robe forever. Because here's the thing: when you get stuck in a mindset of defeat, your business suffers too. Sure, failure might be tough on your ego, but your ego isn't what moves your business forward. What moves your business forward is picking yourself back up and learning from your experience.

So why am I telling you this humiliating story? Because this chapter is all about stepping up to the plate as a business owner. And if you're doing it right, you're going to be trying a lot of things. Some will work . . . but others? Well, they *really won't*. If you believe that every business misstep means you're a failure, you're going to be finished before you begin.

When you're starting out, you should *expect* to experience hardship. It's part of the journey. You're going to lose money; you're going to have launches that flop and content that goes nowhere despite the hours you put into it. It's part of the gig. It does not mean that something is fundamentally wrong with you or that you're not cut out to be an entrepreneur. It doesn't mean you can't create a life and business that fulfills you and makes an impact in this world. It just means you're human.

It doesn't always come easily. But having gone through it myself, I can assure you that it does become easier with time. So here's your pep talk: Failure is temporary. It's the only way you'll know what to improve for next time. You've got to pick yourself up, identify your lesson, learn from it, and then make a plan to try again. And if you get right with failure now, the process will be a whole lot easier later.

The ultimate lesson I learned from that first failed launch was that I *can* make money online. It wasn't the amount of money I had hoped to make, but once you learn how to make $100, you can make $1,000. Once you make $1,000, you can make $100,000. The path is guaranteed to be messy and imperfect, but I promise you, it's worth it.

Even though you're pretty far down the path toward becoming your own boss at this point, I still think it's important to pause for a moment to commit or recommit to the decision.

You wouldn't have gotten this far if you didn't have a calling to become your own boss, create your own schedule, break through the financial glass ceiling, make an impact in the lives of others, and create a business based on *you*. And now you're at the threshold, about to make one of the most important decisions any business owner makes: What type of offer will you be giving the world? And while I believe there's a business model for everyone, the truth is that the only way the strategies I'm about to share will work is if you're committed to the life and business that you know, deep in your heart, you were meant to have.

I've seen it time and time again with my students. When they're on the fence, with one foot in and one foot out, letting their fears hold them back from jumping in head first, it shows in their business. They never quite nail down what their Ideal Customer Avatar needs or show up for them in any consistent way. Their email list plateaus and their engagement across channels peters out. They stop trying new things out of a fear of failing. They get discouraged, falling into a self-fulfilling cycle of imposter syndrome and comparisonitis. And their business never takes off.

If, on the other hand, you're committed to turning a corner and letting your desire be bigger than your limiting beliefs, the future is wide open. Every day I see my students take the exact journey you're taking. They're often tentative at first, unsure if they can really do it. There are *so many* unknowns when they're just starting out, it's no wonder things are a little shaky at first. But those that stick through the hard times, take their failures as lessons, and keep moving forward eventually generate enough revenue in their businesses to live a life they love.

When you want it that bad, magic happens. And that is exactly what I want for you. So let's do this. Let's figure out the offer you're making, and then let's go make some money.

BUSINESS MODELS THAT WORK

Revenue is the lifeblood of any business. But figuring out how to make money doing what you love can seem like an impossible task. That's why I'm going to outline three tried-and-true revenue strategies you can use to start making money in your business. Read through them all and then decide which resonates with you most as a starting point.

Just like lead magnets and social media platforms, you don't need to do all of them at once. (Do you sense a theme?) In fact, I encourage you to start with one business model and, if you want to, build from there. Keep in mind that these are jumping-off points, and you'll need to customize them so they work for you, your business, and your audience. But I do want you to commit to trying at least one of them, and I want you to commit to going all-in.

Without further ado, here are the three top strategies I recommend for new entrepreneurs.

Revenue Strategy #1:
Coaching or Consulting Sessions

The first strategy I want you to consider for making money is to offer consulting, one-on-one sessions, or group coaching sessions in an area you have that 10 percent edge in. This strategy is perfect if you have specific knowledge, and you already have or can easily create a system for teaching others what you know.

To give you some ideas, here's a brief list of the kind of things I've seen entrepreneurs successfully teach others in the online space:

- Dog training
- Home organization
- Reigniting the fire in your marriage
- Food prepping
- Organic gardening
- Meditation
- Makeup tips and tricks
- Web design
- Illustrated journaling
- Building furniture
- Wine pairing
- Needlepoint
- Marketing for travel business owners
- Wedding planning
- Credit repair
- Real estate
- Industry-specific foreign language
- Profitable blogging
- Hitting your child's milestones
- Launching a book using social media (just make sure you've actually done it before!)

And this is just scratching the surface—I could literally go on forever.

Now, how do you make money using that knowledge? You offer limited in person or virtual spots for consulting services, one-on-one coaching, or group coaching sessions. Consulting refers to using your knowledge to consult with, or guide, a client (which could be a company or person) on your area of expertise. One-on-one coaching refers to working directly with one other person to teach them the specific skill that you have. Group coaching is teaching multiple people at once.

There are benefits and drawbacks to each approach. With consulting and one-on-one coaching, you are giving your client or student more focused time, so you can charge more, but you're limited in terms of the number of people you can coach or consult with, since there are only so many hours in the day. With group sessions, you can reach more people in the same amount of time, but you typically charge less for each participant since the experience isn't as intimate.

Whether you choose consulting or coaching, you'll need to get your content organized into a step-by-step process before you meet with your new students (and you can use the Post-it Party exercise from Chapter 4 to guide you). A lot of what you'll cover will depend on the clients or students you're working with and their individual circumstances, so you'll want to be flexible and tailor your approach to the specific client or group you're working with. At the same time, your clients are paying you to clearly and efficiently transmit the knowledge you have, so it's important to organize your thoughts and have a system ready to teach them.

Don't have a system in place already? No problem. Take some time to think back to when you were first learning this skill and write out every step you took to achieve the knowledge you'll be teaching in your coaching or consulting sessions. You don't need to put everything in order right now, just get it down on the page. Think of it as a course curriculum that you're going to drip out one session at a time.

With that in mind, don't forget to include practical exercises in addition to theory! Are there techniques, practices, habits, or tools that helped you on your journey? Anything that will help your clients or students integrate the learning into their own lives and businesses should be there, including your own story of success and that of any other students, clients, or customers you've already worked with.

For example, let's say you help small business owners put systems in place to track and measure their numbers. Your first step might be to tell your own story of starting a small business and what it was like before you had tracking systems in place—and then how things improved once you got them. Then help them determine which metrics they should be measuring in their business by asking them to answer a specific set of clarifying questions. The next step might be to help them create a scorecard or dashboard that features all of the most important metrics in one place, along with your favorite software options. Then you might offer a process for making informed decisions based on the numbers they've identified. Maybe you have a specific recommendation for how often to revisit the numbers, including when they take a turn for the worse.

Don't worry about making each step perfect at this point. You just want to get a rough framework down on paper, knowing you can edit and refine the process later.

Once you've brainstormed all your steps to transformation, you'll want to put them in the specific order needed to achieve that transformation. You may discover that a couple of the steps should be flip-flopped, or that you want to include a few more sub-steps within each part of the process, or that you forgot to include a specific story that will help your clients or students grasp a key concept better. But keep in mind that the more you teach the material, the more refined it will get.

Your clients will tell you what's working, what's not working, and how you can make it better. And I really want to encourage you to try not to see this feedback as failure. Instead see it as important information you were paid to learn that will benefit all of your coaching clients from this point on.

Revenue Strategy #2: Service-Based Work

The second strategy is to take your "you" factor and apply it in real life by offering your customers a service they really need. For example, if you know how to create personalized budgets, you can work one-on-one to customize financial plans for couples. If you've created a delicious breakfast jar all the moms talk about at preschool drop-off, you can make premade jars for the kids at school. If you have experience in fashion styling, you can offer in-home wardrobe consultations.

Or if you're like my friend Danika Brysha, you can offer ready-to-eat, clean, and locally sourced meals. Danika was living in a tiny New York City apartment and working as a plus-size model when she embarked on her self-care journey. After a few months in her new, healthy lifestyle, she was feeling great—but due to her weight loss, she started losing modeling gigs. So she started Model Meals, sharing the same meals she'd been making herself with friends around the city. She eventually moved back home to Southern California and relaunched the company with two business partners, serving premade organic meals to thousands. She took what she knew how to do and offered it as a service to others who were looking for the same results she'd gotten.

As opposed to coaching, where you teach others how to do something for themselves, with a service-based business you do it *for* them. Service-based businesses often require additional considerations, from investing in inventory (for example, if you're making breakfast jars you'll need containers and the foods that go in them) to creating multiple offers to meet the needs of different clients (maybe you offer one personalized budget package for individual clients and another for families).

And if you're already thinking long-term—which, congrats, is the sign of a true boss—it's important to note that a service-based business can be harder to scale or expand. After all, there's only one of you and only so many hours in a day to provide your product or service. That doesn't mean you can't eventually go big, only that you might need more resources to do so.

Revenue Strategy #3:
Build a Workshop Course

The third strategy—and my personal favorite—is to create an online course. This is the bread and butter of my business. In fact, I have an entire digital course that teaches you how to create and promote your own digital course. (I know . . . It's very meta.)

Digital courses come in all shapes and sizes. Some are longer and more thorough, and others are short and focused on achieving a single goal. When you're just getting started, I recommend beginning with the latter, which I call a "workshop course."

This is a short (typically one-hour) training, delivered live, that solves a problem that's been keeping your audience stuck and bridges the gap from where they are right now (experiencing a struggle or challenge, or having an unfulfilled desire) to helping them get to where they want to be. For example, let's say you teach embroidery and your beginner students are struggling to even finish a project. They would gladly pay to learn the basics like how to thread a needle, transfer a design, and learn a few stitches to get started. Or maybe you're a sleep trainer for parents and you create a newborn workshop to lay the foundation for healthy sleep habits from the first night they bring their little one home from the hospital.

There are three reasons a live workshop course is a great way to dip your toes into the online business arena. First, it gives you and your audience each a quick win. Not only are you helping your audience achieve a desired result fast but you're also creating an asset that you can use in perpetuity to generate an injection of cash. Creating and launching this type of online product will help you see what you're capable of—specifically, that you *can* make money online. And since the price point for a workshop course is typically under a hundred dollars, the barrier to entry for your audience is not too high for them to take a chance on you.

The second reason I love a workshop course is that it's a great "baby step." Through your launch efforts and your new paying customers, it allows you to make a little bit of money while you test the digital course waters and continue growing your email list, all with bigger launches in mind for the future.

Of all the different types of digital courses, it's the easiest to create, so if your to-do list is already starting to overwhelm you, this won't add too much stress. It doesn't require an extensive marketing campaign to sell, and unlike a full-blown digital course, it's only one short training, where there is less content to create.

And finally, a workshop course is an incredibly effective way to turn your email subscribers into raving customers by giving them a taste of what you have to offer. Soon they'll be coming back to see if you can help them take the *next* step of a more substantial investment in your services.

Because online course creation is my passion and my top strategy, I'm going to devote the entirety of the next chapter to walking you through the process, so stay tuned! But if you know you want to start with Strategy #1 (coaching or consulting) or Strategy #2 (a service), I'll walk you through two important steps to getting those offers up and running: pricing your offer and announcing it to the world.

1. PRICE YOUR OFFER

Whether you're looking to do consulting or coaching sessions, or service-based work, it's best to keep the pricing simple. You'll first want to do some research on the going market rates for what you'll be offering. Look at what others in your industry are charging, do a quick Google search for similar services in your local community, or ask your Ideal Customer Avatar what they would expect to pay for a service or product like yours.

Once you have a good baseline, you can use a simple formula to determine your price. I'll go through a few variables you'll need to plug in, but you can play with them to see what feels best for you.

First, you'll need to set a reasonable monthly revenue goal for yourself. It may seem counterintuitive to start here, but ultimately you're starting this business to design the life you want to live, right? So let's design something that will get you excited! Maybe you're starting with a side hustle and just want to make enough to finally take that vacation or to cover your mortgage. On the other hand, you may want to ramp straight up to a part-time salary or, eventually, full-time compensation. Either way is great, but for now just take note of the number you're hoping to make per month.

Once you know your revenue goal, you'll need to decide which type of offering you're making. Will you be consulting with one company or coaching one person at a time, doing a group session with five students, or providing a service? From there, you can do the math to determine how many clients you'll aim for, and at what price point per client, in order to make the revenue goal you noted earlier.

Let me give you two different examples.

Example #1

Let's say you have a full-time job and you're looking to start something on the side, with the goal of leaving your nine-to-five once your business is up and running. You've decided to work with busy moms to help create custom meal plans for their toddlers. You've built a simple survey for parents to fill out, which makes creating the plans more streamlined on your end. It takes you about an hour per client, per week, and you can commit to providing this service to five clients at a time.

As you're getting started, your monthly revenue goal is $1,500. You would use the following formula to decide how much to charge for each meal plan:

5 plans per week x 4 weeks per month x $X per plan = $1,500/month

In this example, you would need to charge $75 per customized meal plan to reach your goal. If that feels like too much, or not enough, you can adjust the numbers to adjust your pricing.

Perhaps you look at your schedule and realize you could find time to do seven to eight plans per week. Then you would only need to charge $50 to reach your goal. On the other hand, you may decide that while you're in start-up mode your revenue is not the top priority—what's most important is delighting your early clients with a top-notch service and a price point that makes it an easy yes. So you may decide to lower your monthly goal to $1,000, meaning you can stick to just five clients but still charge them just $50 per week.

Example #2

Now let's say you want to go part-time at your job so you can start consulting with small businesses on their PR strategies. You've already got interested clients, so you know you'll be able to fill 20 hours per week. To cover taxes and business expenses, you also know you want to bring in about $8,000 per month.

You would use the following formula to calculate how much to charge your clients per hour:

20 hours per week x 4 weeks per month x $X per hour = $8,000/month

In this example, you would need to charge your clients $100 per hour to reach your revenue goal. But perhaps you know your audience well enough to know they would be very willing to pay $150 per hour for your services. In that case you could minimize the number of hours you work to 14 hours a week instead of 20 and you'd still make

$8,000. Alternatively, you could increase your revenue goal to $12,000.

There's no right or wrong answer when it comes to pricing. Play around and see what works best for you, your goals, your audience, and the service or transformation you're offering. It's important to remember that even after you go out with an offer, you're not stuck with that price point forever.

I've changed the pricing on almost every offer I've ever made. Sometimes that means changing the offer itself, adding value or changing the deliverable, but nothing is ever set in stone. Don't be afraid to start somewhere and refine from there.

2. SHARE YOUR NEW OFFER WITH THE WORLD

Once you've determined what you're going to offer and how much you'll be charging, you're ready to get the word out. Luckily, you've got the Internet on your side. Your social media platforms are the place to begin. You can announce your offer on the platform you identified in Chapter 10, or anywhere you've started to gather a following. And now that you've gotten your email list up and running—even if it's just your friends and family at this point—you'll want to write to them too. Don't forget to ask them to share your opportunity with anyone else they know who might be interested, since referrals and word of mouth are always the best form of marketing.

Not sure what to say? Let me give you a fill-in-the-blank template of what you might post on Instagram (along with an eye-catching photo):

Are you up for a riddle? Here it goes . . . (10 points if you know the answer)

What's *[insert adjective or phrase describing your product or service]*, *[insert adjective or phrase describing your product or service]*, and *[insert adjective or phrase describing your product or service]*?

Any guesses? The answer is . . . *[explain your product or service and list some of the powerful benefits your Ideal Customer Avatar will experience by working with you—get them curious and excited!]*

I've actually . . . *[explain how you've accomplished the answer above, and why you're qualified to teach on this subject or provide this service]*. And now, I'm sharing my secrets to successfully *[insert the transformation or goal your sessions are based on]*—but only with a select few.

Want in?

I have *[number of openings available]* open spots for *[one-on-one coaching / group training / consulting / service]* with yours truly.

In these sessions, you're going to learn *[list a few things they'll learn]* and you'll walk away with *[list the transformation they'll experience]*.

You deserve to *[the no-brainer reason they should sign up]*.

If you're ready to *[list another transformation or pain point they'll overcome]*, direct message me for more info. These spots are filling up fast so don't wait. I'll see you in my DMs!

Not sure you can freestyle your own post? I've got you! Visit the Appendix on page 258 for a sample of this social media post with the blanks filled in, as well as a fill-in-the-blank email announcement.

DO THE WORK: RESEARCH REVENUE MODELS

After all the hard work you've put in up front—identifying your niche, finding your audience, building your website, creating content, growing your email list, and developing your social presence—it's time to choose your revenue model. Will it be coaching or consulting? Will you be providing a service? Or will you try my personal favorite, creating a workshop course?

While it doesn't matter where you start, and you can test drive all three strategies over time, it's just important to start somewhere. And the best place to do that is with a little research. Go to your favorite social media account (or maybe even look across a few platforms), and identify 20 businesses or entrepreneurs you follow. Then create an actual list—whether it's in a Google Doc, your journal, or the notes app in your phone—and answer the following questions about *each* business:

- What are they selling? Is it a digital course? A membership? A coaching program? A service? A physical product? A book?

- Do they have multiple product offerings?

- Are they a personal brand, a business brand, or an influencer brand? For example, Amy Porterfield, Inc., (personal brand) versus Spanx (business brand) versus the Kardashians (influencer brand).

- Are they affiliated or partnering with anyone else—meaning are they promoting a product or service for another business? For example, your favorite beauty blogger sharing their morning skin-care products or a podcast host you listen to regularly promoting a new book.

Once you have your full list, spend 15 minutes evaluating what you just learned. Grab a highlighter and highlight the business models that speak to you the most. Which did you see on your list—consulting, individual coaching, group coaching, service, online course? Which were you drawn to as you were going through the accounts?

And remember, the goal here is not to have a journey without bumps. In fact, the inevitable bumps are an important part of the learning process. Just because you follow a business online and they have a social media presence doesn't automatically mean that model is profitable. You never know how successful someone is, or the bumps *they're* experiencing, until you're inside the business.

What matters is that you stay focused, leverage the lessons you learn along the way, and use them to grow. If you do, they will make you and your business stronger and more resilient than you can even imagine.

Any of these models will get your business off the ground and start bringing in revenue—a huge milestone worth celebrating!—so you can't go wrong. If an online course or workshop piqued your interest, let's explore what's truly possible by walking through the exact steps it takes to create a revenue-generating asset.

Chapter 12

Launch a Revenue-Generating Asset
The 5-Step Process to Create a Workshop Course

auren was a successful personal stylist with a waiting list of clients wanting to hire her to expertly style their wardrobe for them. But a typical day consisted of what felt like endless mall runs, shopping for clients, and lugging clothing racks to every corner of town—not to mention sitting for hours in LA's infamous traffic jams. Burnout was on the horizon, until Lauren got an idea. What if she stopped styling her clients in person and turned her business into an online program where she would teach women how to look their best by styling *themselves*?

Almost immediately, Lauren was hit with an overwhelming feeling of doubt. Her clients were paying her to do the work for them—for a service, not an information product. Would they even want to take a course that could teach them how to be their *own* personal stylist when they could just hire someone to do it for them?

Despite her concerns, Lauren mustered up the courage to try. She created a course she called Personal Style University. She has since welcomed 326 students and hundreds of thousands in revenue, and she has never looked back. With over 10 million views on YouTube, Google named her as one of their #WomenToWatch, and she's been featured in publications like *Marie Claire, Vogue, The New York Times, The Hollywood Reporter,* and *The Wall Street Journal.*

Fast-forward to a day in the life of Lauren now, and you'll find a woman who is doing what she loves—helping women look their best—without having to set foot in a department store. She's been able to scale her business in a way that feels right for her, including launching a membership site and publishing three books. What started as an idea riddled with doubt has turned into a seven-figure business and a ripple effect of impact, with her students going on to work as stylists for celebrities like Beyoncé, Lady Gaga, and Madonna. There's no reason this same success cannot happen for you!

THE 5-STEP PROCESS TO CREATE, PROMOTE, AND DELIVER YOUR WORKSHOP COURSE

At the end of every year, I host an Annual Promo Planning workshop where I teach my students how to plan their promotional calendar for the upcoming year. Even though I have a suite of more in-depth digital courses, I love offering this short, no-brainer option for my audience. It's a product I created a few years ago, and I've been able to reuse it every year with a few updates, generating additional revenue in my business with minimal effort. It's a topic I'm passionate about, and I followed a simple five-step process to get it up and running. Let's walk through these steps together to see how you can create a workshop course for your business.

Step 1: Make Three Key Decisions

There are three key decisions you need to make about your workshop course up front: the topic, delivery date and time, and price point and revenue goals. Having these decisions made will help you move more quickly and easily through the rest of the steps, so I recommend taking a moment to really think through them.

Key Decision #1: Topic

The one decision that will put everything else into motion is to get clear on *what* you're going to teach in your workshop course. And the best way to do so is to ask yourself the following question:

> *What is the one thing I know my audience needs that I can confidently help them with?*

Let's say you are a career coach for women who are reentering the workplace after staying home to raise their children. You know that the *one thing* they struggle with first is their résumé. They don't know what to include, what not to include, and how to handle the gap from when they were out of the workforce. To address this pressing need, you could create a résumé-building workshop that walks your attendees through each section of their résumé. You could include layout templates, sample content, and copy direction. The outcome of the workshop would be a résumé your students feel proud of and can confidently submit for a job they really want.

Or let's say you are a hairstylist and you've been researching and testing new lead generation strategies to bring in new clients, resulting in a huge increase in business for the past year. Now you want to help other stylists to do what you've done. You could create a workshop called "How to Get 10 More Clients This Month Using This Single Paid Ad Strategy." This topic is helpful, exciting, and allows your audience to take an important step toward growing their clientele.

If you still can't come up with a topic or maybe you have *too many* ideas, try polling your email list or posting a question on your social media platform of choice. You could list a few ideas and ask your audience to vote on which one they'd be most likely to sign up for. Or you could pose a question and pull your topic from the responses or comments you get.

When you include your audience right from the start, they become a part of your workshop creation journey. And when they feel like they are a part of your journey, they're more likely to buy when you get to step three!

Keep in mind that your workshop course isn't the time to go all-out and teach everything you know. The goal is to get new customers into your world and to give them an idea of what's possible if they work with you. You don't want to overwhelm them at the start. Instead, you want to be short and sweet to help them get a single result or quick win that will move them along to the next step of their journey.

Key Decision #2: Date and Time

The next decision is to choose a date and time to deliver your workshop. This is a relatively quick and easy decision, but one you want to make—and then stick to. The date and time will impact your back-end setup as well as your promotion phase. Since you teach this workshop to a live audience rather than prerecording it, you want to determine a time that is likely to work for your Ideal Customer Avatar. For example, if your students are teachers, you know they're exhausted on weeknights. It may be best to plan your workshop for a weekend instead. Or if, like the previous example, your students are hairstylists, you might want to choose a Monday, when many salons are closed.

Key Decision #3: Price and Revenue Goals

Finally, you want to determine the price point for your workshop and set revenue goals for yourself. This process is similar to what we discussed about pricing your service or coaching package in the previous chapter, but there are fewer variables to consider.

As before, I recommend doing research to see what similar online trainings cost or asking your Ideal Customer Avatar what they would expect to pay. For a one-hour workshop, I recommend charging somewhere between $49 to $99, depending on your audience and the promise of your training.

Choosing where your workshop fits on the pricing scale begins with figuring out what the learning is worth to the student. For example, skills that are simpler and will appeal to "beginners" might warrant a lower price point.

Say you're a potter, and you're teaching newbies the basics of a pottery wheel. You might be pricing your audience out at the $49 level. Or you might imagine many students will be just dipping a toe in the pottery waters, and they may not be committed enough to pay $49. In that case, you might choose an even lower price point. Just make sure that your decision is based on your observations and understanding of your Ideal Customer Avatar and is not rooted in fear of your own self-worth. Remember, growth comes when you are most uncomfortable.

On the other end of the spectrum, consider charging more if your workshop offers a more impactful transformation, especially if you're teaching professionals a technique that is likely to increase their own revenue.

Let's say you're a doula and you've created a business working with pregnant women to plan their postpartum recovery. You know lots of other doulas and midwives would be interested in this kind of a side business, but they don't know where to start. You could offer a workshop course just for doulas and midwives, teaching them strategies to find a consistent client base in such a high-turnover industry. In this case you could likely charge more than $99, because the information you'll be offering could easily translate into thousands of dollars of annual revenue.

Once you have your price point worked out, it's time to set a revenue goal for yourself. Revenue goals are important because you want to have a target to be working toward and a way to measure the success of your launch. In all of my launches, I set three goals for my business: a good, a great, and a "holy cow!" revenue goal. Here's what that might look like if your workshop is $100:

- The "Good" Goal: $1,000—You need to sell 10 seats. You've *totally* got this!

- The "Great" Goal: $2,000—You need to sell 20 seats. It's doable but a stretch. Let's do it!

- The "Holy Cow!" Goal: $3,000—You need to sell 30 seats. Amaze yourself!

These are only suggested goals; by all means, do you! If you want to set your goals higher, based on the strength and engagement of your current email list and your social media audience size, the sky's the limit! If you feel like 10 students is a stretch for you at this moment in time, feel free to turn down the dial. The idea is for your goal to be motivating and exciting, not a disappointment in the making.

Step 2: Set Up Your
Behind-the-Scenes Technology

I know, I know. As soon as I trot out the *T*-word, everyone runs for cover! But you will have to set up a little bit of back-end technology to make your workshop come alive. The good news is that the process is simple if you know what you're doing. And to help you out, I've broken it down into four easy action steps:

1. Decide how you'll connect with your students

2. Create a web page where they can buy your workshop

3. Send an email to confirm their purchase

4. Decide if you'll offer a replay of the live training

Tech Action #1: Decide How You'll Connect with Your Students

Obviously, your audience will need to have access to your live workshop once they've purchased entry. There are many options available to get your training into the hands and onto the screens of your students, but the easiest way is by creating a webinar link using video teleconferencing software like Zoom. Such platforms allow you to present from any device, speak directly into the camera or use slides, and give your students access to join from anywhere and on any device simply by clicking on a link you provide.

Depending on how advanced you want to get, you could also create a private community like a Facebook group and deliver your workshop directly inside the group via Facebook Live. You could even embed a livestream video on your website. While that option takes a bit more technical know-how, it means you have total control over the look and feel of the student's experience.

Tech Action #2: Create a Web Page Where They Can Buy Your Workshop

Next, you need a sales page, a shoppable landing page where someone can purchase the transformational workshop you're putting on. For bigger, more expensive courses, a sales page can become very complex, requiring different sections like FAQs, detailed success stories, and bonuses. But one of the great things about this type of workshop course is that you can choose to keep it incredibly simple, including just the basics of what your potential customers need to know:

- The title and topic of your workshop course

- The big picture of what they are going to learn if they sign up

- A clear understanding of what's in it for them (the benefits they will get from attending)

- Objection rebuttals (where you address any concerns your Ideal Customer Avatar might have that could keep them from signing up)

- The date and time

- The price

- Social proof such as testimonials from paying customers or recommendations from colleagues (If you don't have any yet, that's okay! It's something to work toward!)

- A clear call to action (i.e., to enroll in the work-shop course)

You can create the sales page the same way you cre-ated your lead magnet opt-in page: by using a landing page template from your email service provider or website plat-form. The difference here is that you need to make the sales page shoppable, meaning you have to include a way for your potential customers to purchase.

On the back end, you will need to select a payment processing platform for your students to input their credit card information and pay for the workshop. There are sev-eral options to do this, and many are very simple.

For example, your email service provider may offer e-commerce integration. Alternatively you could use your payment processing platform to create a checkout page, which you can link to directly on your sales page. (If you go this route, just make sure your payment processing platform integrates with your email service provider, so your paying customers get added to your email list.)

Most shopping cart platforms provide knowledge data-bases and tech tutorials with step-by-step instructions for how to do this, so make sure to check out the options your software offers. And if all of this has your head spinning and you'd rather focus your efforts elsewhere, consider hir-ing a web savvy admin to help set up the back-end tech-nology for you.

For an example of a simple sales page and corresponding checkout page, and recommendations for payment processing platforms, shopping cart platforms, and how to find tech experts to help, visit the online resource hub at www.twoweeksnoticebook.com/resources.

Tech Action #3: Send an Email to Confirm Their Purchase

Once a student registers for the workshop (congrats—pop that bubbly and celebrate!) you want them to receive a confirmation email with their registration details. This email can be short and simple, letting them know their money was received and giving them the login details to access the live training. This email should be sent automatically when someone inputs their credit card information rather than you having to manually email them, and it can easily be set up by connecting your payment processing platform to your email service provider. For a sample workshop confirmation email, check out the Appendix on page 261.

Tech Action #4: Decide If You'll Offer a Replay of the Live Training

Lastly, you'll need to decide whether or not you want to offer a replay video of your live training for those who missed the event or would like to watch again. The benefit of a replay is that it may result in more customers, as those who know the time doesn't work for them might still register and plan to watch the replay.

Because you're offering more ways to access your workshop, you can consider increasing your price slightly—how much more you charge will depend on your original price and how long the replay is available for. The downsides are that you might have fewer people attending live if they know there will be a recording available and there's a little more work on the back end, as you'll need to figure out how they can access the replay.

If you decide to offer the replay, you have a few options:

- Upload the video to a cloud storage service, like Dropbox or Google Drive, set your access settings to view only, and send your students a link to the video in a post-workshop email.

- If you have a closed community set up for your workshop course participants, like a private Facebook group, host your replay video there.

- Embed the replay video in a standalone, password-protected web page on your site and send the URL and passcode to your students via email.

Step 3: Design a Marketing Plan

In order to get potential customers to your sales page to purchase your workshop course, you'll need to promote the course to your audience and direct them to the sales page where they can enroll. The actions you take to do so constitute your *marketing plan*.

For a workshop course, I recommend promoting your course for one week leading up to the actual day of the live workshop. When you are creating your marketing plan, there are two main promotion strategies you'll want to consider: social media and email.

Marketing Strategy #1: Social Media Promotion

Promoting on social media can look like a blog post on LinkedIn with a topic that aligns with the workshop topic, an Instagram Story, a promo post on Pinterest, or a short Facebook Live. All of these are excellent ways to get the word out about your workshop.

Keep your posts short, sweet, and engaging. For example, let your audience know the three most important things your workshop covers and why it's a must that they grab a seat. You want to get them excited enough that they click the link in the post (or, on some platforms, the link in your bio) that will take them to your sales page for all the details. If you're planning to do video promotion, it's a good idea to choose a URL for your sales page that is easy to say and remember—for example, amyporterfield.com/workshop.

I like to focus on what I call the Who-What-Why of your workshop when promoting on social media:

- **Who** is your workshop absolutely perfect for? Talk directly to your Ideal Customer Avatar.

- **What** can your attendee expect to take away from the workshop? Write down a few concrete benefits they'll get and incorporate the list into your post when you promote on different social channels.

- **Why** did you create this workshop? Share the backstory of your decision to teach on this topic. Give some interesting details and insights into why this training is so valuable.

Need more inspiration? Check out a sample Instagram workshop promo post in the Appendix on page 263.

Marketing Strategy #2: Email Promotion

This is the moment to leverage that email list you've been working so hard to grow! Remember, your subscribers have already raised their hand and said they are interested in what you have to offer. So even if your list is still modest, you can take heart that these are your "warm" leads, and they will convert into sales most easily and frequently. Hopefully you've been nurturing their interest every week with valuable content, so they're primed and ready to take the next step with you: this workshop!

I recommend sending three emails: the "invite email" plus two preworkshop emails for registrants. The invite email lets your fans know the workshop is coming up and highlights the transformation they can expect to see after taking it. The goal of the invite email is to pique the reader's interest and create the excitement that will drive them toward registering. You'll want to include your workshop title, a quick overview of what the course covers, why it should matter to your subscribers (making sure to touch on any challenges, obstacles, or desires the workshop will address), the date and time, the price, and a link to your sales page.

I suggest sending this invite email a week before you deliver your workshop. Then two to three days later, get the list of subscribers who haven't yet opened the first invite—your email service provider will be tracking which subscribers have opened the email and which have not— and *resend them the exact same email with a new subject line!* This way, you have another chance to capture their attention. Visit the Appendix on page 265 for an example of a workshop invite email.

Once your students sign up, you'll want to continue to engage with them to ensure they *show up*. You'd think the fact that they've paid to attend would be enough to get them to their computer at the right day and time, but you would be *wrong*! Life intervenes, we forget, we get inertia and want to keep binge-watching our favorite show . . . there are a million reasons people don't show up to the workshops they've paid good money for.

This is where the two preworkshop emails come in. These emails don't need to be as in-depth as your invite email, since the recipients are already registered. But the goal is to keep the excitement going, reminding them of all the great content you're going to deliver. I suggest sending one email 24 hours before your live training and one the day of—maybe even 15 minutes before—so they can just click the link and join.

It's always a good idea to make it as easy as possible for your students by giving them all the details they need at the top of their inbox. Include a subject line that's obvious, like "Your XYZ Workshop Is Going LIVE Today! (Access Details Inside)."

Here's a chart to recap the email sequence:

	Email #1: Invitation	Email #1b: Invitation Resend	Email #2: Prework-shop 1	Email #3: Prework-shop 2
What to Include:	Explain what your workshop is about and highlight the transformation it will help your Ideal Customer Avatar attain	Exact same email as #1 with a new subject line	Create excitement around what you're going to deliver and make it easy for your students by giving them all the details they need at the top of their inbox	Create excitement around what you're going to deliver and make it easy for your students by giving them all the details they need at the top of their inbox

	Email #1: Invitation	Email #1b: Invitation Resend	Email #2: Preworkshop 1	Email #3: Preworkshop 2
Who to Send to:	Entire email list (and/or friends and family, and ask them to forward to anyone they think would be interested)	Only send to those who didn't open email #1	Anyone who purchased your workshop	Anyone who purchased your workshop
When to Send:	One week before your workshop	Two to three days after email #1	24 hours before the workshop	Morning of the workshop

Step 4: Create the Training Content

Once you have your tech set up and you're actively promoting your workshop course, it's time to dial in the content you plan to teach. The good news? This is only a one-hour training and the final 15 to 20 minutes can be Q&A. You'll be pleasantly surprised at how quickly the content will come together.

Speaking of a Q&A, I highly recommend doing a short session at the end of your training. It's an easy transition to wind down your workshop, provides immense value to your students, and builds a connection with your audience. Have one to three questions preselected to kick things off in case it takes a minute or two to start getting questions from the live audience. (People can be shy!)

A good place to start is to have the most frequently asked questions you already get written down. You can start by saying, "To get us going, let me answer a couple of questions you might be asking yourself right now." This gives you confidence moving into the Q&A section of your workshop, especially if you have a quieter audience.

I used this strategy when I was brand new and had a small audience and it always made me feel at ease, knowing I had some questions ready to go in case all I heard was crickets when I finished my training. Trust me—it's better to be prepared and not use these questions, than to *need* them and not have them at your fingertips!

I also suggest teaching from an outline rather than writing out a full script. Now, I know that doing a live workshop for the first time can be scary (especially for us introverts!), and preparing a script so that you know exactly what you want to say and can stay on track feels like a smart move. But here's the thing: trying to stick to a script can make you sound robotic and emotionless, which in turn can make your audience feel less connected to you.

If you come across as comfortable (even if you feel *all* the nerves on the inside), your audience will trust you more and relax as you teach them what they signed up to learn. Instead of using a script that you read word for word—which by the way, would also require you to master the art of reading off a teleprompter, something I *still* struggle with!—I recommend speaking casually to your audience, like you're talking to a friend. And if you need a little more certainty than that, try scripting the first five minutes of your introduction and using an outline from there. This allows you to feel prepared when you'll be the most nervous.

To create your workshop content outline, let's bring back the Post-it Party strategy from Chapter 4 (page 71).

It's simple and incredibly effective. Just in case you need a refresher, here are the steps:

1. **Grab Your Supplies:** Grab a stack of Post-it notes and Sharpie and go somewhere with a blank canvas—e.g., a wall, mirror, or window—so you can stick all your Post-it notes up and see them clearly.

2. **Brainstorm:** Set a timer for 15 minutes and write down every workshop-related idea, story, piece of content, insight, or action item that comes to mind. If it makes sense to your topic, consider adding a couple of quick-hitting exercises for your students to do—maybe it's having them make a decision or write a response to a prompt you provide. Remember, there's no editing in the brainstorming phase! Every idea gets a Post-it note.

3. **Organize Your Outline:** Once your timer goes off, take an additional five minutes to sort through your Post-its. Take the ones you want to use and organize them by phases or steps. This will help you begin to visualize the flow and sequence of how you want to teach your content. When you're done, you'll be looking at the first draft of your workshop outline!

4. **Fine-Tune Your Outline:** Now it's time to open up a Google or Word doc and transfer your Post-it notes to the page. Take an hour or two to fine-tune and expand on your outline—move things around, delete things, add in some new ideas and begin to flesh out your ideas, giving more details and specifics. Remember, because you are only teaching for about 45 minutes, and your students

are looking for a quick fix, it's critical not to over-whelm them with too much content. It's equally critical to have fun! Teach some core content while telling stories, using examples, and engaging your students.

5. **Final Review:** Once you've dialed in your outline, I recommend stepping away for a few hours (or even a couple of days) to give your mind a little time to let it all settle in. Then come back to it for a final review to smooth out things and make sure you've nailed the flow. Think about the results you promised your students—are you sure this content will get them there? If not, make some changes. But then call it done!

Create a Visual Aid

If you want to go the extra step and your content warrants it, you may want to include a visual aid in your presentation. This could be something like sharing a slide deck from your screen or delivering your training while standing in front of a whiteboard that allows you to write out key concepts or sketch examples. Or maybe your workshop topic is about how to execute a specific craft and you might prefer to have your camera set up so you can talk directly to the camera for part of your workshop and show your attendees a more tactical demonstration for the other part.

If you're considering a slide deck, keep your slides simple—there is no need to get fancy here. You can use a program like Canva or Google Slides to create your slides. Your content is what counts the most.

I recommend having slides that name your most important teaching points, which both helps with your audience's digestion of the material and keeps you on track as you teach. The less text you include on your slides the better. You want your attendees listening to what you're saying, not reading through your slides the entire time. And I always like to switch out my slide every minute or so of talking—otherwise, you can lose your audience.

Pro tip: Always get a second set of eyes on your slides before the workshop to make sure there aren't any typos. Even if you just ask a friend for help, you'll be glad you did. And keep in mind that there's no one way to present your content, so choose the best way for you and your students and run with it!

Practice, Practice, Practice

The final thing I want you to do before your live workshop is to practice, practice, and then practice a little more. I'll admit that practicing a workshop is not my favorite way to spend an afternoon, but I'm always *so* very glad that I did it.

When you do a practice run, all the way through from start to finish, you start to see the areas that looked good on paper but don't work in reality. Wouldn't you rather know this *before* you teach the workshop? Even if you feel super confident in your content, I beg you not to skip this part! I'm always most nervous in the first few minutes of my training, so I practice my opening a few extra times. That way I can show up with confidence and be fully present with my students.

If there's any area that's tripping you up more than others, spend a little more time there so you get comfortable before you're live.

Step 5: Deliver the Workshop and Wrap Up

At this point, you've planned out the workshop content, set everything up on the back end, and filled your training with paying customers. Now it's go time! On the day and time promised, you're going to deliver your live workshop course to your students. Let me share a few tips for going live to ensure everything runs smoothly:

- Do a tech test run 24 to 48 hours in advance where you test out all the technology you will need to go live. It will calm your nerves and allow you to work out any pesky tech gremlins in advance.

- On the day of your workshop, go live 10 minutes early. You can make sure the technology is working properly, and if all is going well, you can chat with your students before you dive in.

- Remember that it's perfectly normal to get nervous when you go live, but just think about *why* you created the workshop content in the first place. You want to help your students overcome an obstacle, learn something new, or work through a process so they can move forward. You've promised to help your students achieve a transformation with your training—now it's time to wow them. You've got this!

Once your workshop has been delivered, and after you do a little happy dance (and if you're me, enjoy a skinny margarita) it's time to wrap things up with a final, post-workshop email to your students. The goal of this email is to thank your students for attending and to give them any final details you'd like them to know. If you promised to give them access to your replay, this is where you would send them access details. For a sample of a post-workshop email, visit the Appendix (page 269).

DO THE WORK: MAKE YOUR KEY WORKSHOP DECISIONS

Now that I've walked you through the entire five-step workshop process, let's go back to the beginning and start making those key decisions. Put a timer on for 15 minutes and answer the following questions:

1. What is one thing you know your audience needs that you can confidently help them with? (And re-member, if you have more than one thing, spend this time creating a post on social media or writing an email to ask your audience what they want to learn the most!)

2. What date and time will you deliver the workshop? What is the best time for your Ideal Customer Avatar?

3. What price will you charge?

4. What are your "Good," "Great," and "Holy Cow!" revenue goals?

Taking the step of creating your very first workshop proves that you're really going for it—you're making yourself known and beginning to carve out your own space online.

If you're thinking, *But what if it bombs? What if no one buys?*, I'm here to tell you that it *might* in fact bomb. And it might not. If you're going to think about the worst-case scenario, then you better give equal air time to the best-case scenario too. *What if a bunch of people buy? What if it's a big success?*

Did you know that Walt Disney was fired from the *Kansas City Star* because his editor felt he "lacked imagination and had no good ideas"? How about the fact that when Marilyn Monroe was trying to start her career, modeling agencies told her she should consider becoming a secretary? Steve Jobs was pushed out of the company he had co-founded because the board felt he was wasting the company's resources working on expensive projects that did not have enough potential.

In other words, not everyone will understand your value or see your greatness. But here's the good news: It doesn't matter. You don't need everyone to pay attention and you certainly don't need everyone to like you. Focus on creating awesome content for your community. Be consistent and show up, even when you're scared. Teach from the heart. These are the tried-and-true principles that lead to success.

Chapter 13

Ready, Set, Boss

Once upon a time, a woman rallied all the courage she could muster and started her own business. One day she was an employee in a windowless cubicle, hitting the glass ceiling at every turn, and the very next day she was her own boss, calling the shots and making more money than she'd ever imagined. Sure, in the beginning there were some roadblocks and challenges, but soon everything fell into place and she was living exactly the life she had envisioned. Because she owned her own business and became her own boss, life was rainbows and unicorns forever after. The end.

Well . . . not *quite*!

The truth is, becoming your own boss is not always going to feel like a fairy tale. It's a journey that takes time, perseverance, a thick skin, and a determined heart. You don't just quit your job on a Tuesday and wake up Wednesday feeling like the "boss babe" you see all over Instagram. Unbossing happens decision by decision, experience by experience. Over and over again you'll be forced to redefine your values, update your operating principles, and learn what it means to be the leader you want to be.

In fact, when you are new to being a boss, you *will* make some missteps. We can't know what we don't know, and there are about a million opportunities to make a mistake. Oftentimes what we don't know only reveals itself when we fall into its trap. How do I know this? Because yours truly has fallen into just about every boss trap imaginable. These challenging situations are common to all new bosses everywhere—but they don't have to end your journey, as long as you know how to maneuver them.

So consider this chapter my final gift to you: a heads-up about the top five most common boss traps I see—illustrated by my own flops and failures; how fun!—and my best advice for how you can remedy them and stay steady on the road toward your dream.

BOSS TRAP #1: LETTING YOUR CLIENTS BOSS YOU AROUND

When I started my first service-based business providing social media marketing for small companies, I said yes to every opportunity that came my way, mostly out of fear of missing out or not making enough money on my own. Soon I had eight clients, each of whom came with their own set of wildly unrealistic expectations and unmanageable deadlines. And there I was, behaving just as I had in my corporate gig: agreeing to do the impossible, pushing myself harder and harder, and sacrificing my happiness for theirs.

Inevitably, the situation came crashing down, and it was on an airplane tarmac, where I had my laptop in one hand and suitcase in the other. My phone was pinned between my neck and ear, and I was straining to hear my client yell at me about a recent webinar I'd helped him with where the tech had gone terribly wrong. But then he said something I heard loud and clear: "Amy, this will never happen again!"

At that moment, something in me snapped and I knew he was right. And not because I was going to work harder to meet his impossible demands. But because I was *done*.

I may have started my own business, but I was still working for someone else. I was beholden to my clients' needs, wants, and, let's face it, whims. I was having the exact same experience I'd hoped to leave behind when I left my job. Even though I'd had the confidence to venture out on my own, somewhere deep inside I didn't truly believe I was smart enough, strategic enough, or savvy enough to be my own boss.

After working with thousands of women over the last decade, I know I'm not alone here.

Too many self-employed women I encounter are working as if they're still employees. They throw their own boundaries and self-respect out the window in exchange for satisfying their client's every need and want. If you often feel frustrated and resentful of the clients you're working with, it's likely because you are letting them boss you around.

If you have the urge to yell, "Yesssss! This is me!" then the following remedies will help you get out of this boss trap—and keep you from falling into its grip again.

Remedy #1: Put It in Writing

Before you begin working with a client, clearly set the expectations in writing. Talk to your client about the goals of the project, the necessary deliverables, and what "complete" looks like, so that you are both crystal clear on the desired end result. Once you've connected with your client about the details, draft a contract that will be signed by both parties. This way, there are no gray areas. The clearer the expectations, the easier it will be for you to stay on track.

To help you get started, I've included a downloadable contract template in the online resource hub at www.twoweeksnoticebook.com/resources. It's also a good idea to work with a lawyer or a contract specialist to review any contract before you use them with clients.

Remedy #2: Pause before Agreeing to New Tasks

Before volunteering yourself for a new task, commit to pausing. Take a deep breath. Depending on the project and the meeting, someone else may step in and volunteer to take it on. If not, ask your client who they think would be the most appropriate owner of the task. If they suggest you're the right person, let them know you want some time to look at your task list for the project and you'll be back in touch later that day or the next.

It's never the wrong decision to give yourself a little more time. If your client pushes back and wants an immediate answer, you may need to have a heart-to-heart with them—in which case, move on to the next remedy.

Remedy #3: Revisit the Project

If you find yourself taking on too much—and therefore feeling discouraged and resentful—revisit the goals of the project. If the scope has expanded beyond the original agreement (which happens often) it might be time for a "client check-in call." Here you can zoom out together and look at how, when, and where the project goals expanded beyond the original agreement. Then together you can formulate a new plan that will support the added complexity of the project.

The most important thing to remember when you're working with the boss trap of feeling like an employee is that *you* are the boss now. The whole reason you took this leap of faith to create a business and a life that you can be proud of is that you wanted more joy and sovereignty than you can get as an employee. To reach this goal you have to commit to setting the boundaries you need, respecting yourself, and standing up for what is right. If you do, you'll find over time that this trap will disappear, never to be thought about again.

BOSS TRAP #2: THINKING YOU NEED A MAN TO HELP YOU

Time and again I've seen that, in both our personal and professional lives, we women think we aren't good enough or capable enough to do big things on our own. For some of us, that might mean thinking we need a man to help us each step of the way. And by "some of us," I definitely mean *me*. In other words, it's time I tell you about my partnership.

I'm going to be really honest: I wish I didn't have to tell you this story. To say I have mixed emotions about it would be an understatement. But in spite of how painful this experience was, I am hugely grateful for everything it opened up for me—and I hope by telling you the story, you'll be able to avoid making a similar mistake yourself.

About three years into building my online business, I had reached out to one of my colleagues in my mastermind group for help to boost sales in a specific area of my business. He quickly saw a much bigger opportunity—taking all of the offers in my entire company and optimizing them to generate more revenue. With this in mind, he presented a proposal for a 50/50 partnership in my business. And with one quick signature, it was done.

If you're wondering what sort of counsel I sought from mentors about entering into this partnership and how much time I took to think it over, prepare yourself. *It took*

me one night of sleep and I ran the decision by precisely nobody.
I took the business I had started from scratch, the business that was on the cusp of experiencing a million-dollar year, and I gave 50 percent of it to someone I barely knew because he said he saw promise in me.

Looking back, I see that even though I was over the hump of starting my online business and things were truly starting to click for me, I *still* felt like I couldn't do it unless I had a man guiding me and reminding me I was capable. I told myself that if I crashed and burned (a thought I had almost daily) at least someone would be there with me. If I got stuck, I would have someone there (okay, specifically *a man*) to pull me out of the mess. If I didn't know the answers (a common experience), he would know what to do. What I was really saying was, "I am not safe without a man by my side. I am not capable of figuring this out. Letting him lead me will protect me from failure."

From the minute we began working together, the business went to a new level. We quickly created new programs, dialed in our marketing funnels and products, hired our first full-time employee, and grew our email list. By the next year, we were a multimillion-dollar business, and I started to become known as a leading online marketing expert.

But once again, behind the scenes, I was miserable.

I want to be clear here—I have nothing bad to say about my ex-partner. He was smart, strategic, and knew how to make money. And calling in a mentor who had been in my shoes—and had succeeded—was a great idea. But asking for help is a very different thing from believing you need to be *saved*. Or believing that, in order to deserve mentorship on the business journey, you have to give away half of what you've already created.

When a launch didn't go as planned or things felt messy, I looked to him to tell me we were going to be all right. And for years, I worked 60-plus hours a week, never asking him to take on any of the extra work that was burying me. I left our meetings with 20 action items, while he left with just a few. I let him lead, and I resumed the role of yes-girl.

My misery kept growing, until one day I blurted out to a friend, "I'm not happy in my business." She asked about my partnership and I instantly got defensive, "Let's not talk about that. It's an off-limits conversation. There's nothing I can do about it because I'm too far in." She gave me a look and I knew I was avoiding the one thing that was killing me inside.

The light eventually came on: the partnership was no longer working for me—because it had started to feel like *I was working for him*. I had to get out.

The next year was full of tense, awkward, and heated conversations with my business partner. The kind of conversations that make you want to crawl out of your skin. There were lawyers and legal documents, and at every turn, I thought I would lose my business. I thought I had failed, and I blamed myself for the entire mess.

We got to a point where it looked like we would never come to an agreement, and the only way out was to completely dissolve the company. *My* company. It was gut-wrenching, but the pain itself reminded me how right I was to make this shift.

Then one morning I woke up, eyes swollen from incessantly crying the night before, to a completely new thought. *If we have to dissolve the business, that's okay. I will pick things up and do it all over again—but this time, 100 percent on my terms.*

At some point in that difficult and nearly catastrophic year, quietly and without me noticing, my power and confidence had come back. While nothing had changed outwardly, inwardly I was at peace. Within a few days, I felt ready to propose formal mediation, and within a few months, I successfully bought my partner out. I was once again the sole owner of my business.

Within the next year, I took the business from $5 million to over $16 million in revenue. I had finally, officially, and permanently unbossed myself. I was free.

The process of unbossing is a crucial step on your journey to becoming your own boss. Before you make the leap to start your own business and make it a success, you have to let go of the fear of doing it on your own. You have to believe that becoming your own boss is the only way forward. You have to want it badly enough and be willing to lead yourself, no matter the obstacles and challenges ahead. Because beyond those challenges is a world of opportunity, personal growth, and freedom.

In order to help you avoid the "I can't do this by myself" boss trap, I want to give you a few remedies to help you make sure your next move is the right one for you and your business.

Remedy #1: Phone a Friend

If you come across an opportunity that you feel is too good to pass up, particularly if it's a new working relationship or legally binding, take a moment and phone a friend. Call someone you trust and share why you want to do it, running through both the pros and the cons. If you have any concerns or fears, express those too. Taking a moment in advance to evaluate the opportunity with someone you trust can save you years of heartache. (PS: If you have the urge to skip this step, it's likely because you know there are red flags and you don't want to face them. How do I know this? Because I've lived it!)

Remedy #2: Seek Professional Guidance

My goal is to help you avoid any business partnerships, arrangements, or opportunities that do not serve you at the highest level. To be clear, I'm not saying that *any* business partnership with a man is the wrong one. What I am saying is that I want you to make sure you're signing up for the *right reasons*. In looking at my deeper motivations—and separating what's good for the business from what's simply familiar and comfortable to me—nothing has helped more than being in therapy.

Sometimes we just can't see what's holding us back on our own. But talking things out with a professional, sharing our innermost fears and desires with someone we trust, allows us to better understand why we make the choices we do.

With a therapist's guidance, I've been able to recognize my self-limiting patterns and habits, get more clear on who I am, and start to speak up for what I want and need. It's been one of the most important catalysts for breakthroughs in both my personal and professional lives, and I couldn't recommend it more highly.

BOSS TRAP #3: STAYING SAFE THROUGH SELF-SABOTAGE

I am a pro at self-sabotage. It's part of my DNA. The instant something good happens, I can turn it on its head, finding a way to dull its light in a nanosecond. I am not proud of this; in fact, I'm downright mortified to admit it. I could easily list off 20 self-sabotaging experiences I've had since starting my business. In fact, this book you're holding now was one of them.

When I landed my book deal, the terms were beyond my wildest dreams. I was speechless. Once I found the words to share the details with my husband, we celebrated for approximately 10 minutes—and then I proceeded to torture myself for the first two months as I wrote the book. I told myself daily that I was not a writer, that I did not have what it takes to write a real book, and that the wonderful publisher who gave me this opportunity had obviously lost their mind. Those fears and doubts turned into horrible, agonizing writing days, which turned into more anxiety than I had ever experienced in my life.

But here's the thing: *I did that to myself.* I took something amazing and flipped it into something bad in a matter of minutes. I suspect the reason I find it easier to torture myself than to believe in myself is that I've lived my whole life by the belief that I am not good enough, that I don't deserve to be happy, and that I am not capable of greatness. I've struggled with a lifelong fear that if I get something good, it can be taken away. (Dang, this stuff runs deep!) So when something incredibly wonderful came my way, my self-esteem was too low to believe I deserved it, and so instead, I self-sabotaged.

Eventually, I did manage to snap out of it and move into a much better place. Having a deadline helped! I didn't have a choice; I was on the hook for a draft. So I had to take a deep breath and *write*. I started reminding myself daily that I would not have been given this opportunity if I was not ready for it. I began focusing on what I was grateful for more and more each day, and slowly but surely my writing days became easier, and dare I say it, enjoyable!

Starting a business is no small undertaking. And you are about to embark on something big. Huge, in fact. Being your own boss means the buck stops on your desk. Too many times I've seen women—talented women, passionate women, women who were born to be running their own companies—self-sabotaging their way right back into a *J-O-B*. I don't want that for you!

I want you to courageously step into the vision you have for yourself, understanding that courage + time = confidence. I want you to stay the course, while confidence is taking shape behind the scenes.

With that in mind, let me share some of the self-sabotage archetypes I see in the people around me (and, frankly, in the mirror!) to see if any of them sound familiar to you. Recognizing yourself in any of these descriptions is a big win, because the number one remedy for the trap of self-sabotage is *awareness*.

Archetype #1: The Procrastinator

If you find yourself putting off exciting projects or specific action items that you know you want to take, then you may be self-sabotaging through procrastination. Leaving unchecked tasks on your to-do list only creates more stress and worry as the deadline approaches. Underneath procrastination is often a belief that we aren't deserving or we can't actually achieve what we really, truly want. When you're feeling deadline dread, take a deeper look at yourself and ask if you're falling into this self-sabotaging trap.

Archetype #2: The Overthinker

Constantly delaying decisions? Running through every single scenario that could or might happen? You may be embodying the self-sabotaging archetype of the Overthinker. This is tricky because it slows your business down *and* can chip away at your confidence. Ruminating ad nauseum often means we don't yet trust ourselves to make the "right" decision.

Start paying attention to the little successes you see in your everyday life, noting them as often as you note your failures. And remember the times in the past when you fell on your face and successfully picked yourself up again. Being in business for yourself means you'll make lots of mistakes, but progress can only be made when you trust that you'll bounce back when you do.

Archetype #3: The Self-Critic

If you're one of the beat-yourself-up types, you may be self-sabotaging through self-criticism. Nobody is 100 percent terrible at everything, so start focusing on the things you do well. Ignoring these positive aspects of yourself and obsessing about how you are flawed or wrong will only block your creativity, energy, and flow. You *are* worthy of the opportunities in front of you. The only thing that stands between you and the success you want is your own belief that you're not good enough to have it.

BOSS TRAP #4: MISTAKING EXCITEMENT FOR GOOD BUSINESS

When I finally had my first successful digital course launch, I didn't want to lose the momentum. Naturally, I thought, *I'd better do more!* Other successful online business owners were doing masterminds, memberships, social media challenges, marketing funnels, live events, podcasts, interviews—and my mind exploded.

For a brief moment, I thought I should try it all. Heck, I'd had success with digital courses, so why not give these other strategies a spin? I wanted to try something new, something fun! But then one of my accountability partners stepped in and gave me what would become for me a multimillion-dollar piece of advice.

"Whoa! Hold on just a second," she said. "You just had your first successful launch. Before you add more, do a rinse and repeat."

"Huh?" I asked, feeling the excitement drain away. I had honestly never considered taking the same product and doing the same launch again a few months later, after making a few key improvements.

My accountability partner pointed out that I had already done the initial hard work, and so this next promotion would be easier and likely even more profitable. I took her advice and have never looked back. Now I teach all of my students the "rinse and repeat method."

Overwhelming yourself with too many projects, strategies, and opportunities—especially when you are just starting out—is a surefire way to end up in the fetal position, thinking maybe your *J-O-B* wasn't *that* bad. (PS: Make no mistake, it was!) To ensure you don't take on too much out of sheer excitement, here are a few remedies to help you prioritize your business and focus on what *really* matters.

Remedy #1: Iterate before Starting from Scratch

Something about the entrepreneurial personality craves variety. Starting a new initiative gives you that addictive hit of dopamine. The challenge with this habit is that contrary to how it feels, starting over from scratch slows you down. No project is perfect on the first try, so if you're always launching something new, you're likely to be providing only lackluster results for your audience. Instead, give your products—and your business—time to fully mature. Use your energy to optimize what's already working, and you'll end up getting better results with less work.

Remedy #2: Calm Your Mind by Documenting All New Ideas

If you are a multipassionate entrepreneur, you likely have lots of ideas swirling around in your head at any given moment. And your initial impulse may be to start scheduling *all* of them. Proceed with caution!

Contrary to what your entrepreneurial brain is telling you, not every idea deserves equal attention. The idea that deserves the most attention is the one you are working on right now. Stay in your lane and focus on the goals you've already committed to. When a new idea pops in your head, add it to a special "Notes" section on your phone so you won't forget it. And when the time comes where you have the space and bandwidth to start a new project, use this list for inspiration.

Remedy #3: Stay in Your Lane

FOMO—or fear of missing out—is a very common challenge for many entrepreneurs. When you see other business owners trying new trends and creating new types of offers, you may feel like you have to do the same or you'll be left behind.

The challenge with FOMO is that it directs your attention toward what you *aren't* doing, causing you to lose sight of what's already in the works. It can take you off track and keep you from the commitments you've already made, which means sunken expenses and lost revenue.

To be a successful entrepreneur, you can't let outside influences grab your attention at every turn. So each time you feel that sense of FOMO, keep your head down, take the next step on the to-do list you already have, and remind yourself that you can do anything you want to do in your business—you just can't do it all at once!

BOSS TRAP #5: SUPERWOMAN SYNDROME

After six years into my business, I'd hired independent contractors to help me get the work done but did not have any full-time employees of my own. I was nearing the point of burnout, ending my working day with 10 or more action items still unchecked on my to-do list. The workload was too much!

The moment I took off my Superwoman cape was when I hired Chloe to be my full-time marketing project manager. In the beginning I was hesitant to let go of some of my most important work, mistakenly thinking I was the only person who would do it right. But slowly and over time, Chloe became an essential part of the business—freeing me up to be more strategic and intentional with how I spent my time. Chloe became my right hand, working closely with me for seven long years, helping me take the business to incredible new heights.

Letting go of my Superwoman cape allowed me to grow the business while becoming a stronger leader and entrepreneur along the way. It remains one of the best business decisions I've ever made.

For new bosses, trying to do it on your own is very normal. It can feel scary and risky to commit to paying someone else to help you. But take it from me, overworking and overstressing yourself does no good for your business. It results in missed opportunities and misery. So here are my remedies to the boss trap of holding on to that cape for dear life.

Remedy #1: Get Honest with Yourself

If you prefer to forge ahead alone, keeping every task on your own plate, ask yourself *why*. What are you afraid might happen if you asked for help? Have you asked for help in the past and not received it? Do you think asking for help will make others think you are weak?

Examining our hesitancy to get the help we need often unlocks unconscious beliefs that are keeping us stuck in a number of different ways. So take some time, pick up your journal, call your best friend or your therapist, and see what hidden motivations you can uncover when you commit to being honest with yourself.

Remedy #2: Get Clarity about Where You Need Help the Most

One way to clarify where you could use help is to look at the goals you've set for yourself. What are you working toward right now? What campaigns or new initiatives do you have coming up?

Now I want you to think about what tasks you need to be doing right now in order to meet those goals. Go ahead—write them down. Then ask yourself: "What's one thing I could ask for help with right now that would ease my workload and give me more peace?" Choosing one thing—just one—can open the doorway to getting the support you've been needing for a very long time.

Remedy #3: Remember Your *Why*

Take a moment and remind yourself why you want to start your own business. Think about the freedom, the opportunities, the rewards that you know are waiting for you. Really get in touch with your desires here.

Now imagine if you could get to all of these wonderful things even *faster*. Would you be willing to put down your Superwoman cape in exchange for a shortcut to your dream? If so, it's time to invite others to help you. When you're the only one doing all the work, there's a cap on how much you can do. Bringing on help can double or triple the productivity and speed with which you realize your dreams. It can also increase your revenue over time.

The long and the short of it is that keeping all the tasks on your own plate is a rookie move. There is no badge of honor in doing it all on your own! In fact, playing Superwoman will slow you down and create stress and overwhelm, which will keep you trapped. If you want to grow your business more effectively and quickly, then invite others in to help.

JUST TAKE ONE STEP

No matter where you are along your entrepreneurial journey—whether you've just decided to give notice, just gone out on your own, or just decided to take your business to a new level—the only question to ask is, "What's my next step?" As long as you're moving, you're *moving forward*. That's my hope for you.

One of the simplest but most important pieces of advice I could leave you with is to let the process of taking your next step—whatever it may be—be easy. How you do that is to choose one single action item and focus only on that until it's done. Schedule some Tiger Time if you need it, find a quiet spot, and complete an action item that meets you where you are in your journey right now.

Here are some starter ideas, based on different stages of the unbossing journey:

- **If you still have a full-time job** and have just started considering starting your own business, start by declaring your *why*.

- **If you know you want to take the leap** but you need some added motivation to make it happen, choose your date and put it on a sticky note.

- **If you've already gone out on your own,** or started a side hustle, but you're struggling to get any traction, start by defining your Ideal Customer Avatar.

- **If you already know who you want to serve** but can't seem to turn your followers into an actual email list, start by creating a lead magnet.

Now choose a symbolic goal, something that you'll take action on once you're your own boss and have the money to make it happen. Maybe it's a special purchase, a bucket list vacation, or a heroic donation to a charity that matters to you. Would it be an expensive handbag? A family trip you've always dreamed of but could never afford? Maybe you'll finally remodel your house and get those wood floors and marble countertops you've been dying to get. Or maybe you'll make a donation to the animal shelter where you found your beloved pet. What will it be?

This is your time. You're ready to dive into an ocean of possibility. The light is green. Go now. You have absolutely *everything* you need to create your online business—just get started and remember to trust the process. Progress beats perfection, and every action you take is bringing you closer to your goals.

You are needed by your audience. You have lives to change. You have people to serve. Your impact is needed in this world. Never quit on your dreams. All you've got to do is go out there and make it happen, boss!

Appendix
Sample Scripts, Posts, and Emails

CHAPTER 2

Own Your Exit Scripts

Script 1: Conversation with a Loved One or Intimate Partner

Use this script to communicate with anyone in your life who may not understand why you want to make a change—and therefore may struggle to support your decision. This script will guide you as you share with your loved one or partner your desires, your current challenges, and your vision for the future. The script will help you stay clear and on-topic as you outline your future steps.

Fill-in-the-Blank Script:

> "Let me start by saying, I'm **[insert how you're feeling about having this conversation, e.g., *nervous, scared, hesitant*]** to have this conversation. Not because I'm not confident in my decision, but because it means so much that you support me in what I'm about to tell you.

> "Don't worry, I didn't **[share an example of something that will bring levity to the conversation, e.g., *buy a new car and max out the credit card*]**. What I want to talk about is my decision to **[unapologetically state what you've decided to do, e.g., *start an online business with the goal of quitting my job by the end of the year*]**. If that feels scary to you, trust me, it's a whole lot scarier for me! But I'm doing this because **[explain why you've made this decision, e.g., *I can't envision myself ever finding true happiness and fulfillment if I keep doing what I'm doing*]**.

"I don't have it all figured out, but I've thought about this long and hard, and I'd rather try and fail than never try at all. I want to do this for myself, for us, for all the people who need what I have to offer. The thing is, I know my odds of failure will be dramatically diminished if I have your support in this. Will you help me find the courage to make it happen?"

Script 2: Conversation with a Friend or Co-worker

Use this script to communicate with friends or co-workers who are questioning your decision to make a change. This one's for the naysayers, those who'll project all their own insecurities on you. Be direct and confident in your decision, without apologizing or overly communicating for the sake of wanting approval. With this script you are especially communicating, *I'd appreciate it if you could support me even if you don't get me.* The goal is for you to protect your heart, your dreams, and your boundaries.

Fill-in-the-Blank Script:

"You know, there are lots of things in life that we don't really understand but that we also don't question because we know they're important. Do you know the mathematical formula to explain gravity? I know I don't, and it doesn't matter. What matters is gravity keeps our feet glued to the earth.

"You might not understand my desire to **[insert what it is you've decided to do, e.g., *quit my stable, well-paying job to start a business teaching art*** *online*], but it doesn't matter. What matters is that it's important to me and that I'm committed to making this happen.

"I didn't make this choice lightly and I know there's risk involved. I also know you're trying to keep me safe by sharing your opinion on my decision, but what I need from you is support and I ask that you keep your doubts to yourself.

"I appreciate your concern for me, but I'm not turning back. I'm committed to making this happen and one thing that will help me do that is encouragement—or at the very least, quiet acceptance—from the people in my life. Can I count you as one of those people?"

Script 3: Email to a Questioning Friend or Co-worker

Below is the script for an email that you can tweak and make your own to let your family, friends, or co-workers know about your big life change. It is intended to communicate your decision and your boundaries around their opinions—*even before they share them*. The goal is the same as the script above. Once again you are communicating, *I'd appreciate it if you could support me even if you don't get me.*

Fill-in-the-Blank Script:

Hey **[Name]**,

I've always appreciated your friendship and love working with you. As you know, I've decided to

[insert what it is you've decided to do, e.g., *quit my stable, well-paying job to explore teaching art online*] and I know that probably came as a shock.

I also know that you care about me and my future, and that sometimes care can show up disguised as doubt and discouragement.

Before that ever happens, I want you to know I love hearing your opinion and feedback, but I'd appreciate it if you keep it positive. I'm committed to moving forward with this and need all the support and encouragement I can get from my well-meaning friends like you.

Yours truly,

[Your Name]

CHAPTER 11

Sample Social Media Post

Are you up for a riddle? Here it goes . . . (10 points if you know the answer)

What sharpens your attention, reduces stress, increases compassion, and improves your mental health and your relationships? Plus, it requires ZERO experience and takes less time than it takes to watch an episode of your favorite show?

Any guesses? The answer, unsurprisingly, is meditation. You've heard of all the benefits and you've probably said to yourself . . . "I *should* meditate, but who's got time for that and where would I even start?"

I used to have the same questions. But with the help of some amazing teachers, I started meditating three years ago. To say that my life has gotten MUCH better since then, in just about every way, would be an understatement!

I want the same for you! So I've created a set of guided meditations that are perfect for anyone who's brand new to the practice that can be used every single day as a way to reconnect and enjoy the process without feeling like you're doing it wrong. And now I'm sharing my secrets on how even the busiest among us can find five minutes a day to get more focused and less stressed—but only with a select few.

Want in?

I have 10 open spots for individual coaching with yours truly.

In these sessions, you're going to learn the number one reason holding you back from adding meditation to your routine, how this simple practice can improve your personal *and* professional life, and you'll walk away with a daily meditation you can implement right away.

You deserve to experience all the physical and mental benefits meditation has to offer.

If you're ready to be pleasantly surprised by the difference this short practice can make, direct message me for more info. These spots are filling up fast so don't wait. I'll see you in my DMs!

CHAPTER 11
Promo Email Announcement Template

Hey **[First Name]**,

Does **[what your coaching sessions or services will help them achieve]** seem like something you **[describe what's held them back from getting the kind of results you promise in the past]**?

It sure used to feel that way for me. Especially because when I did **[action you're asking them to take]**, it always felt like **[describe how you used to struggle too]**. **[Elaborate on the pain you experienced before finding the solution]**. Can you relate?

If the answer is yes, I want you to know that **[give them hope, share how you shifted out of that struggle]**. **[Share how you discovered the solution and what that made possible for you]**. I want the same for you.

I'm offering only **[number of openings available]** spots for **[one-on-one coaching / group training / consulting / service]** that will take the guesswork out of **[describe what you teach]** by **[how you make it so doable]**.

If you're craving more **[list a few benefits your offer will help them achieve]** that sticks even when **[a typical limitation or excuse that this will help them surpass]**, then one of my **[coaching spots / services]** has your name on it!

Click here to respond to this email to secure a spot and **[offer a benefit they'll receive through your services and link this entire sentence to your email address]**.

Because of the **[describe the impact your offer could make for others in your target market]**, I want to invite you to share this resource with any **[describe the type of people you want them to share it with]** you think might benefit.

Simply forward this email to your friends, family, and colleagues, and spread the **[describe the feeling they will receive, e.g., *calm and happy*]** vibes that this opportunity is sure to bring.

Again, simply press "reply" to secure a **[one-on-one coaching session / group training / services]** with yours truly before they're all gone!

[Signoff]

CHAPTER 12
Automated Confirmation Email Template

Subject: YES! Your spot in the **[Workshop Name]** Workshop is locked in!

Email Copy:

Hi there, **[First Name]**! I'm over the moon excited that you've secured your virtual seat in my upcoming live workshop. I hope you're as excited as I am to dive into all things **[describe what will be covered in the workshop]**!

Next step? Make sure to mark your calendar with the date and time of the workshop and plan to show up live.

Yes, the training will be recorded and you'll get access to the replay, but there's something special about the live aspect. Not only will you get to ask me questions in real time, but when you show up live, you are more likely to implement quickly and get the results you're after.

Here are the details:

When: **[Date]** at **[time (include time zone)]**

Length: 1 hour

Where: Online! The link to join live will be sent to you 24 hours in advance.

Until then, start thinking big as you look toward **[describe the goal or transformation they will achieve after attending your workshop]**. We've got some major dreams to fulfill!

[Signoff]

PS: Before our training, I want you to **[include any**

exercises, instructions, homework, or research they should complete before coming to the workshop].
PPS: As a reminder, I'll send you a link to access the live workshop on **[date]** 24 hours in advance of go time! It's going to be an awesome training and I can't wait to share it with you!

CHAPTER 12

Sample Workshop Instagram Promo Post Example

Truth: Your physical environment has a HUGE impact on your internal environment.
So when I work 1:1 with my clients to pare down their closets to the key style items that fit their vibe and serve multiple purposes . . .

I'm not surprised by this added benefit they get: *PEACE OF MIND*

It might sound like a stretch to say that clearing out your closet (or wardrobe . . . or the pile of clothes on your sofa) can have such a huge impact on your mental well-being.

But hear me out—

Our minds have a certain capacity every day. And once that's wiped?

Well, you're wiped. And it looks like this . . .

Constant guilt over the unfolded laundry you threw on the floor—*I just washed it and now it's getting wrinkled, but I'm exhausted so screw it.*

Decision fatigue from all the choices you're making throughout the day—*Should I pack the kids PB&J or cut-up veggies? Will I be cold if I leave this cardigan at home even if it ruins my outfit?*

Knowing you've got tons of clothes, but . . . still going for that same blouse and skinny jeans combo you always wear.

Sound familiar?

The truth is . . . it wears on you. (And not in the fun way that cashmere wears.)

I think we both know you're ready for a shift.

That's where my NEW workshop "Cut the Clutter—Create the Capsule" comes in. This workshop is *aaall* about getting your wardrobe in order, clearing the mess, and creating your perfect capsule wardrobe.

Oh, yeah . . . AND looking really freakin' good doing it.

Here's what you'll learn in this workshop:

- What a capsule wardrobe is and how to create one

- How to identify your core style and select the pieces that match

- How to *actually* clear out the clutter (no, it's not

just indiscriminately throwing out your clothes)

- THE best way to organize your pieces so you can take the brain work out of looking incredible every day

If you're currently staring at a laundry basket full of old tops you haven't worn in years (how did they end up in the laundry basket though??) and jeans that don't fit right . . .

Click here → **URL.com/workshop** to grab your seat inside Cut the Clutter—Create the Capsule right now!

It's only $97 and it kicks off on March 1st at 4 P.M. ET.

See you there!

CHAPTER 12

Workshop Invite Email Example

Subject: [NEW TRAINING] Learn Exactly How to Plan Your Business Goals in the New Year

Email Copy:

I know what it's like to let another year slip by . . . and realize you're *still* not where you want to be in your business.

Maybe you didn't reach your revenue goals.

Or you never wound up creating that new product.

Or you just couldn't dig yourself out from under the avalanche of client work long enough to sell those offers you were SO excited about.

Hey, I get it. And I've been there too.

Sending you a BIG hug, and a reminder to give yourself a little grace. Running a business is tough, and you're doing an awesome job. <3

But I know letting another year fly by might make you wonder if you're "cut out" for this entrepreneurship thing.

Or that maybe you should just give in, and stay doing 1:1 work forever, stuck on the time-for-dollars hamster wheel. (At least you're making money, right?)

Or maybe you should just continue working a full-time gig and burning that midnight oil, because at least you're hustlin', right? Ummmm, nooooo.

Here's the good news: in this very moment, you have the power to break the cycle and make this next year your most profitable year yet.

All it takes is . . . a little strategic planning.

YES, even if you don't have a product or service to sell (yet!).

YES, even if you feel like everything's been made or sold before (it hasn't), or that there's so much competition there's no room for you (there absolutely is).

YES, even if promoting yourself feels totally over-whelming, or so far none of your promos have reached your desired goals.

So let's get one thing straight: if you're ready to make this next year THE year you actually achieve those amazing dreams of yours . . .

I'm ready for YOU.

On November 20, at 10 A.M. PST, I'm running a brand-spankin'-new LIVE workshop, where I'll pull back the curtain on how I plan out every single year of my business, to reach my goals without hustling my life away.

I'll let you in on a little secret:

Planning for my business annually has been an essential part of how I've been able to go from "newbie entrepreneur" to growing a successful business.

And now, I'll show you exactly how I do it with you—step by super-fun step.

You can declare your goals and start mapping out your major projects with my help, and get ALL my profitable planning secrets—which you can use forever—for a one-time investment of just $97.

Quick note—<u>This is early-bird pricing that increases THIS Friday—take advantage of it now!</u>

Inside this LIVE workshop, complete with Q&A at the end, I'll walk you through:

- The EXACT steps I work through each year to plan out my annual and quarterly goals—including ALL the brainstorming exercises and processes I use.

- The magic trick to setting your financial goals (I'm obsessed with this one—because it challenges you to dream BIGGER).

- A game-changing formula for crunching the numbers, and connecting your offers and promotions directly to your $$ goals.

- The little-known secret I use to create my promotional calendar—including the trick for building in the perfect amount of white space so you don't come off too "sales-y" with your audience.

- . . . And so much more.

Isn't it high time you felt like you knew exactly what you were doing in your business?

(Not that throwing spaghetti at the wall isn't fun!)

But I want to help you skip the learning curve, and start making big, confident moves—and moolah—ASAP.

I promise: it's not as hard as you think.

But let me prove that to you!

Click here to learn more about the workshop and enroll—**the price increases THIS FRIDAY, so take advantage of the early-bird pricing before it's too late!**

[Signoff]

PS: I'm convinced this is YOUR year. You're going to want to hit the ground running the minute you ring in the new year. <u>This live training will ensure you make that happen.</u>

CHAPTER 12

Post Workshop Email Example

Subject: Wowza! That training might go down in history . . .

Email Copy:

Hey there, **[First Name]**. If you joined us live for the workshop training, then you already know it was pretty epic. We covered A LOT. If your hand hurts from taking copious notes, make sure to take some time to ice it down today. ;)

If you missed it, no worries. As promised, the training was recorded and it's available and waiting for you **[link to access replay]** (make sure to use the password: **[password]** to access).

If you know me, surely you had to know I was also going to include a **[include name and link to any additional resources, e.g., *a PDF guide you prepared for your attendees*]** for you to use along with the workshop.

So don't wait! Make your way over <u>here</u> today to watch the replay and dive into the training. I just know you are going to love it.

Before I go, I want to give you one challenge. After you watch the training, DM me on Instagram (I'm **[Instagram handle]**) and tell me one takeaway that you will implement in the next 48 hours. I'll be your accountability buddy. :)

I'll be looking forward to hearing from you!

[Signoff]

PS: If you haven't done so already, go <u>here</u> to watch the replay of the workshop training (and use the password: **[password]**). Don't wait—it's too good to put off any longer!

Endnotes

Introduction

1. The World Bank, "Labor force participation rate, female (% of female population ages 15+) (modeled ILO estimate)," data retrieved on February 8, 2022, https://data.worldbank.org /indicator/sl.tlf.cact.fe.zs?end=2019&start=1990&view=chart.

2. "Women CEOs of the S&P 500," Catalyst, last updated March 25, 2022, https://www.catalyst.org/research/women -ceos-of-the-sp-500/#:~:text=*%20Women%20currently%20 hold%2032%20(6.4,at%20those%20S%26P%20500%20 companies.&text=Corie%20Barry%2C%20Best%20Buy%20 Co.%2C%20Inc.

3. Dominic Barton, "It's Time for Companies to Try a New Gender-Equality Playbook," *The Wall Street Journal*, September 27, 2016, https://www.wsj.com/articles/its-time-for-companies-to-try-a-new -gender-equality-playbook-1474963861.

4. "2022 State of the Gender Pay Gap Report," Payscale, accessed March 2022, https://www.payscale.com/research-and-insights/ gender-pay-gap/.

5. Cary Funk and Kim Parker, "Women and Men in STEM Often at Odds Over Workplace Equity," Pew Research Center, last modified January 9, 2018, https://www.pewresearch.org/social -trends/2018/01/09/women-in-stem-see-more-gender -disparities-at-work-especially-those-in-computer-jobs-majority -male-workplaces/.

Chapter 7

1. Edison Research, "The Infinite Dial," Edison Research, last modified March 11, 2021, https://www.edisonresearch.com/ the-infinite-dial-2021-2/.

2. "VNI Complete Forecast Highlights," Cisco, last modified 2016, https://www.cisco.com/c/dam/m/en_us/solutions/service -provider/vni-forecast-highlights/pdf/Global_2021_Forecast _Highlights.pdf.

3. GMI Blogger, "YouTube User Statistics 2022," Global Media Insight, last modified April 18, 2022, https://www .globalmediainsight.com/blog/youtube-users-statistics/.

4. Sofia Cardita and João Tomé, "In 2021, the Internet went

for TikTok, space and beyond," *The Cloudflare Blog*, last modified December 20, 2021, https://blog.cloudflare.com/popular-domains-year-in-review-2021/.

5. Peter Bregman, "How (and Why) to Stop Multitasking," *Harvard Business Review*, May 20, 2010, https://hbr.org/2010/05/how-and-why-to-stop-multitaski#:~:text=In%20reality%2C%20our%20productivity%20goes,ve%20become%20good%20at%20it.

6. David Strayer and Jason Watson, "Supertaskers: Profiles in extraordinary multitasking ability," *Psychonomic Bulletin & Review* 17, no. 4 (August 2010): 479–85, https://pubmed.ncbi.nlm.nih.gov/20702865/.

7. Gloria Mark, "The Cost of Interrupted Work: More Speed and Stress," University of California, Irvine, https://www.ics.uci.edu/~gmark/chi08-mark.pdf.

Chapter 8

1. Direct Marketing Association (DMA) and Demand Metric, "2016 Response Rate Report," July 28, 2016.

Chapter 10

1. Hootsuite and We Are Social, "Digital 2022 Global Overview Report," last modified on January 2022, https://hootsuite.widen.net/s/gqprmtzq6g/digital-2022-global-overview-report.

Acknowledgments

Oh my goodness. What I know for sure is that this book is not my own. It's important that I acknowledge those that supported me on this journey.

I have to start by thanking my hunky husband, Hobie, who literally held our lives together as I navigated my way through this wild ride. I am positive there were days when you asked yourself, "Is this book *really* a good idea?" but you never made it known. You are a saint. As it's always been, I love you more.

Next up, my incredible team. How did I get so lucky? You all have been cheering me on from the beginning and have literally believed in this book far before I ever knew I could make it happen. Thank you for your love, support, and undying dedication to what we do. I need to give a special shout-out to Jenn (Jawes) Goldsmith, who was my sidekick throughout this entire process, from the first word to the last. I could not have done this without you. Your calm demeanor, supportive style, and incredible grasp of our content kept us moving forward. Remember all the times I called you and told you I couldn't do it? I cried, you listened, and then you pushed me back out there. Thank you with all of my heart. Christine Nondorf, my extraordinary executive assistant, who somehow managed me and my schedule (like a freaking boss!) during the busiest season of my life. I don't know how you did it, but girl, you crushed it! Chloe (Cho) Rathje, thank you for diving into this book launch like an absolute pro, even when we had no idea how to launch a book! Knowing you were running this launch allowed me to show up as my best self, and for that I will be forever grateful.

To my family, including, my son Cade, my mom, Beverly, my dad, JB, my stepmom, Shay, my sister Tracie and her family, Rob, Ava, and Lance. You all have been patient and understanding as I've awkwardly navigated this wild world of entrepreneurship. I am forever grateful. You've rolled your eyes while I've recorded videos from the boat on the lake, patiently waited for me to finish my work (I know you've heard me say "I just need five more minutes" a million times!), and calmed my mind when things got tough. Thank you to all of you!

I have some pretty incredible friends who shared their time, graciously shared their wisdom, and loved me when I struggled to love myself. A special shout-out to Jasmine Star, Gabby Bernstein, Jenna Kutcher, Marie Forleo, Jamie Kern Lima, Corinne Crabtree, Mel Robbins, Michael Hyatt, Stu McClaren, Jen Gottlieb, and Julie Solomon—thank you for your time and generous spirit through this special season of my life.

To Scout, my trusted pup. You were at my feet as I wrote every single word of this book. I don't deserve you, but I sure do love you.

To my literary agents at Folio, Scott Hoffman and Steve Troha. You both were class acts throughout this entire process. I told you my hopes for this deal and then you went and blew it out of the water. Your patience, guidance, and support will always be unmatched.

To the team at Hay House—I hit the jackpot with all of you. Many years ago, way before I ever thought about writing a book, Reid Tracy took me to lunch and told me he wanted my book when I was ready to write it. I did not realize he was absolutely serious! It has been incredible to see this all come together. To my editors, Lisa Cheng and

Kelly Notaras, you both found a way to add clarity, finesse, and flow to my drafts, and I know that was not easy. I relied heavily on both of you to walk me through this process and you did so with such patience and grace.

And finally, and most importantly, I want to acknowledge YOU, dear reader. I am your biggest fan. I know you are capable of greatness. I will cheer you on and believe in you with all my heart until you are ready to fully believe in yourself. I love you to the moon and back.

About the Author

AMY PORTERFIELD is an ex–corporate girl turned online marketing expert and CEO of a multimillion-dollar business. During her corporate days, Amy worked with mega-brands like Harley-Davidson, as well as peak performance coach Tony Robbins. After one fateful boardroom meeting and witnessing the lifestyle, financial and work freedom an online business has to offer, Amy developed her 9–to–5 exit plan and never looked back.

Through her bestselling courses and top-ranked marketing podcast *Online Marketing Made Easy*, Amy has helped hundreds of thousands of entrepreneurs turn in their two weeks' notice and trade burnout for freedom, income and impact. Amy's action-by-action teaching style provides aspiring business owners with the tools they need to bypass the overwhelm and build a business they love.

Amy empowers women across the globe to take their futures into their own hands and find professional autonomy, independence, achievement and success far beyond what a corporate glass ceiling would traditionally allow.

Amy's work has been featured in *Forbes, Fast Company*, CNBC, *Business Insider, Entrepreneur* and more. Her company has twice been awarded the Inc. 5000 Award as one of the fastest-growing privately held companies in the United States.

Today, she runs her growing business from Nashville, Tennessee, where she lives with her husband, Hobie, and their Labradoodle, Scout. **www.AmyPorterfield.com**

Hay House Titles of Related Interest

THE SHIFT, the movie,
starring Dr. Wayne W. Dyer
(available as an online streaming video)
www.hayhouse.com/the-shift-movie

* * *

*THE GREATNESS MINDSET: Unlock the Power of Your Mind
and Live Your Best Life Today,* by Lewis Howes

*THE HIGH 5 HABIT: Take Control of Your Life with One
Simple Habit,* by Mel Robbins

*HIGH PERFORMANCE HABITS: How Extraordinary People
Become That Way,* by Brendon Burchard

*MARKET YOUR GENIUS: How to Generate New Leads,
Get Dream Customers, and Create a Loyal Community,*
by Nikki Nash

MOVE THE NEEDLE: Yarns from an Unlikely Entrepreneur,
by Shelley Brander

*YOUR STAND IS YOUR BRAND: How Deciding Who to Be
Will Revolutionize Your Business and Change Your Life,*
by Patrick Gentempo

All of the above are available at www.hayhouse.co.uk

* * *